The SECRETS of High Magic

VINTAGE EDITION

The SECRETS of High Magic

VINTAGE EDITION

Practical instruction in the
occult traditions of high magic, including
tree of life, astrology, tarot, rituals,
alchemic processes, and further
advanced techniques

FRANCIS MELVILLE

BARRON'S

A QUARTO BOOK

Copyright © 2002, 2012, 2024 by Quarto
Publishing plc

Cover © 2024 by Sourcebooks
Cover design by Hannah DiPietro/
Sourcebooks
Cover images © Gorbash Varvara/
Shutterstock, NaokiKim/GettyImages

Internal design © 1998, 2010 & 2024 by
Quarto Publishing plc

Sourcebooks and the colophon are registered
trademarks of Sourcebooks.

This publication is designed to provide
accurate and authoritative information in
regard to the subject matter covered. It is sold
with the understanding that the publisher is
not engaged in rendering legal, accounting, or
other professional service. If legal advice or
other expert assistance is required, the services
of a competent professional person should be
sought. —*From a Declaration of Principles Jointly
Adopted by a Committee of the American Bar
Association and a Committee of Publishers and
Associations*

Published by Sourcebooks
P.O. Box 4410, Naperville, Illinois 60567-4410
(630) 961-3900
sourcebooks.com

ISBN-13: 978-1-7282-9609-8
ISBN-10: 1-7282-9609-9

Library of Congress Control Number:
2011927077

QUA: SMV

Editor & designer: Michelle Pickering
Illustrators: John Woodcock, Carol Woodcock
Art director: Caroline Guest
Indexer: Pamela Ellis
Thanks to: Sarah Marley, Philip Morgan,
Michelle Stamp
Creative director: Moira Clinch
Publisher: Paul Carslake

Originally published as in 2002 in the United
Kingdom by Quarto Publishing plc. This
edition issued based on the hardcover edition
published in 2012 in the United States by
Barron's Educational Services.

Printed and bound in China

OGP 10 9 8 7 6 5 4 3 2 1

CONTENTS

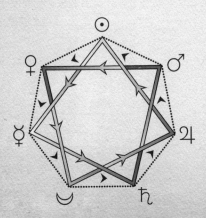

So, you want to be a magician? Or a conjuror or a mage? Well, if you are just looking to dazzle others with clever tricks, you have picked up the wrong book. However, if you are looking to penetrate the deepest mysteries of life, then you may consider yourself an aspiring mage and read on. If you are just window shopping, feel free to stick around—if the time is right, you may choose to get involved.

Introduction

A medieval mage studying the planets and stars.

Getting involved is easy; you just have to say, "I'm in." It is a choice, an act of will, a statement of intent. Involvement is the first key to magic. Once you are involved in something, you become a necessary part of it—it includes you. The more you involve yourself, the greater the reciprocal effect. It is, therefore, wise to acquaint yourself with the basic rules of the game before leaping into the fray.

BE PREPARED
Once you reach a certain stage of involvement, there can be no return to a state of blissful ignorance. High magic reveals awesome dimensions to life that cannot be safely apprehended by weak or fearful individuals—not because these dimensions are of themselves frightening

or malign, but because they demand the capacity to accept profound truth. Dabblers who paddle in the waters of magic can find themselves getting in deeper than they had planned, sucked under by chimerical quicksand or swept along by powerful hidden currents. The aspiring mage should know how to swim before risking these deep and potentially treacherous waters.

KNOW THYSELF

The practice of the magical techniques in this book will lead you into encounters with higher levels of reality, so it is of the utmost importance that you are well grounded. All those who aspire to high magic should be blessed with imagination, but be free from fantasy. Magic is not a cure for maladies of the spirit. Those suffering from neuroses or depression will find such conditions more likely to worsen than improve.

You need to have good equilibrium and be comfortable in your own skin. You must be scrupulously honest with yourself. Any skeletons lurking in the closet are bound to leap out at some stage, so it is a good idea to spend time mentally reviewing the events of your life. In this way, you will be as prepared as possible for whatever emerges.

PROFOUND TRANSFORMATION

Magic demands focus, discipline, tenacity, and courage. If used correctly, the sacred rituals and techniques in this book will generate profound changes that will transform your life on every level. They provide the necessary tools for self-initiation into the higher realms of eternal cosmic reality.

What is high magic?

High magic is both a science and an art. Its roots are ancient, but its techniques continue to evolve and adapt to the conditions of all ages. The aim of magic is to effect changes in both inner and outer reality through the awareness and manipulation of unseen— therefore occult—but powerful forces. The techniques of high magic include:

- *Purification*
- *Meditation*
- *Divination*
- *Kabbalistic exercises*
- *The making of ritual tools*
- *The creation of talismans*
- *The preparation of alchemical elixirs*
- *Conjurations*
- *Angel magic*

Getting Started

High magic can be extraordinarily powerful, so its practice is not to be undertaken lightly. First, you must prepare yourself, laying firm foundations for the great work ahead. Start by preparing an outer temple—a sacred space in which to work—and then concentrate on achieving inner equilibrium. When you feel ready to proceed, you can prepare the magical implements for ritual use.

The great work is nothing less than the achievement of godhood—that is, union with the divine—using the three pillars of high magic—astrology, alchemy, and magic—to do so.

The great work

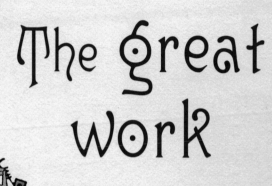

Thoth, the Egyptian Hermes.

High magic is also known as hermetic magic because it is based on the hermetic arts and sciences. These are so-named because they are derived from the teachings of Hermes Trismegistus (thrice greatest Hermes), the many-named genius of magic who mediates between the macrocosm and the microcosm, heaven and earth, the divine and the individual.

THE EGYPTIAN HERMES

The ancient Egyptians knew Hermes as Thoth or Tehuti, the divine personification of wisdom. Portrayed as the ibis-headed scribe of the gods, he was the inventor of hieroglyphics and the patron of the sacred sciences of geometry, mathematics, astronomy, medicine, magic, and alchemy. Thoth exists at every level of being. He serves the gods, but he also preceded them.

Indeed, he brought them into being, for he is the self-creating arch-magician. He has but to name a thing and it springs into life. He is the cosmic alchemist, the inner and outer teacher, the balancing point between all polarities.

THE GREEK HERMES

The Greeks identified Thoth with Hermes the divine messenger, who mediates between heaven above and earth below. He is the ambivalent god of the crossroads, being both guide and trickster and patron of both merchants and thieves.

THE HERMETICA

Hermes Trismegistus is credited with writing *The Hermetica*, or *Corpus Hermeticum*. These texts were once believed to be ancient, but in the seventeenth century it was established that they were written in Alexandria in the first three centuries of the Christian era. They may, however, have been elaborated from much earlier manuscripts. Some of these writings were translated by Arab scholars from Greek and Coptic manuscripts and were introduced into Europe via the Moors of Iberia in the twelfth century. The main body of writings, however, was not translated and distributed in Europe until 1471.

Hermes, the divine messenger of the Greek gods.

TRANSLATING THE HERMETICA

In the fifteenth century, Cosimo de Medici, the great patron of the Florentine Renaissance, instructed philosopher Marsilio Ficino to interrupt his translations of Plato to translate into Latin a Greek set of *The Hermetica* that he had obtained from Byzantium. Cosimo was determined that he should read the legendary writings of Hermes before he died. Ficino did not let him down. The recent development of printing allowed for *The Hermetica*'s swift dispensation throughout Europe.

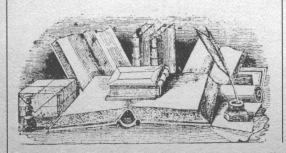

Sixteenth-century drawing of man inscribed in a pentagram with the planetary symbols. Man is the microcosm, reflecting the influence of the universe, or macrocosm.

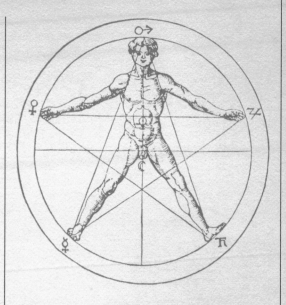

Hermes's great dictum

Hermes Trismegistus's great dictum "as above, so below," with its correlate "as within, so without," summarizes the fundamental hermetic principle that everything in creation is reflected in man.

In tarot, the Magician points a wand toward the heavens and his other hand toward the earth, representing the hermetic dictum "as above, so below."

THE GREAT MIRACLE

The impact of *The Hermetica* on Renaissance philosophy was enormous. Here was an ancient body of theological, magical, and medical writings of extraordinary beauty, intellectual power, and spiritual authority. Jews, Christians, and Muslims could all find confirmations, amplifications, and refinements of their sacred teachings within.

In *The Hermetica*, the creation myth becomes a much richer, more detailed, and expressive allegory—an awesome alchemical process. Hermes describes man as "the great miracle," capable of achieving godhood as an individual by transcending the stages of being that separate him from the divine. Man is dignified as being truly made "in the image of God," being the microcosm that reflects the macrocosm. He therefore has at his disposal all the tools he needs to achieve his divine destiny, should he choose to accept it.

THE WAND OF HERMES

The wand of Hermes, known as the caduceus, provides us with a master key to unlocking our divine potential and making magic. Derived from a Greek word meaning "herald," the caduceus is a key message for humanity. It is a symbol of peace, protection, and healing and is used to this day as a medical symbol. Above all, it is a symbol of unity achieved through the reconciliation of opposites. It appears in many traditions and finds one of its most significant expressions in Indian yoga (see pages 116–119). By working with the caduceus, a magical equilibrium can be achieved that allows us, like Hermes, to sprout wings and ascend to the realms of the gods.

THE CADUCEUS

The caduceus is an ancient symbol. The earliest known version is about 5,000 years old. It consists of two serpents entwined around a central pillar or wand, usually surmounted by a pair of wings. The coupling snakes represent all the opposing principles at play in the manifest universe—male and female, light and dark, yin and yang. The central staff symbolizes the axis between heaven and earth, the microcosm and the macrocosm. The wings represent transcendence or pure universal spirit.

The caduceus borne by Hermes in his role as celestial herald.

You will find it easier to focus your energies and perform your magical operations if you create a sacred space within your home. Establishing this outer temple is an important first step in manifesting your sacred intent.

The outer temple

A small cupboard can be used both as an altar and for storing magical implements when not in use.

If you are fortunate enough to have a spare room in your home that you can designate as your temple, so much the better. If not, section off part of a room with a curtain or screen. The space should be large enough to contain a small table and a chair. The chair should be straight backed, with or without arms, and the right height so that your feet rest flat on the floor and your knees form a right angle. You may also like to include a bed or couch to recline on during certain magical practices.

THE ALTAR
A small table about 2 x 2 ft. (60 x 60 cm) will work well as an altar. A square shape is ideal, but a rectangular or round table will do. An even better form of altar consists of a small upright cupboard.

The cupboard is convenient for storing away magical implements, candles, and incense. Traditionally, the altar should come up to your belly button. Use a piece of black silk, perhaps with tassels at the corners, as an altar cloth; it should hang at least a third of the way to the floor. Stand the altar in the middle of the room.

CLEANSING

Once you have established the space for your temple, you need to clean it thoroughly. Get down on your knees and scrub if you have to. Chase out the cobwebs and make everything as sparkling and fresh as you can. Then burn some frankincense, myrrh, or sage leaves, blowing the purifying smoke into all the corners, nooks, and crannies to shoo out any stagnant energies. A fresh coat of paint always transforms a room and is well worth the effort and expense. Some mages wash the walls and ceiling with saltwater before painting them. Use pale colors on the walls, unless the room is particularly light, but the ceiling can look superb painted midnight blue with stenciled luminous constellations. Finally, sprinkle some saltwater around the room to discourage unruly critters of all kinds from invading your pristine sacred space.

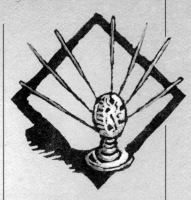

Burn incense and use the aromatic smoke to purify your temple.

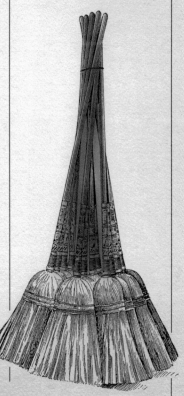

Keep your temple clean, brushing, scrubbing, and dusting thoroughly.

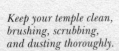

Purify your temple by burning sage leaves instead of incense if you prefer.

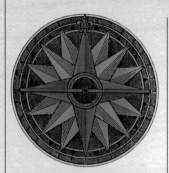

Use a compass to mark the north, south, east, and west of your temple.

BANNERS

It is necessary to establish the orientation of your temple by dividing it into four quarters at the cardinal points north, south, east, and west. Use a compass to do this and mark each quarter by hanging a banner made of cardboard, cloth, or hide. You may wish to decorate the banners with the colors, elemental symbols, and zodiac signs associated with the direction.

MAGICAL ROBES

Wearing a robe that is exclusively reserved for temple and ritual work is a traditional part of being a mage. This can help you achieve the right frame of mind and develop your magical personality—an "alter ego" that transcends your mundane personality. Ideally, you should make the magical robe yourself. This can be of almost any design you like, but keep in mind that freedom of movement is important when practicing high magic.

A long dressing gown is a good model for a magical robe. You could even take apart an old dressing gown—maybe one from a thrift store—to see exactly how to cut the cloth. If you find the prospect of sewing your own robes daunting, the hardest part is probably threading the needle. It is unlikely to be the most difficult task you encounter—patience and determination are key.

CHOOSING YOUR MAGICAL ROBES

Suitable colors

- These include black, white, violet, and cream.
- If your magical work is related to a planet, use its corresponding color (see pages 36–49).

Suitable fabrics

- Use natural materials, such as wool, silk, linen, and cotton.
- Avoid using manmade fibers because they block the subtle energies with which you will be working.

Violet is a suitable color for magical robes, and also corresponds to the Moon.

The four banners

North

White; earth; Capricorn,
Taurus, and Virgo.

South

Red; fire; Aries, Leo,
and Sagittarius.

East

Yellow; air; Libra,
Aquarius, and Gemini.

West

Black; water; Cancer,
Scorpio, and Pisces.

As well as preparing an outer temple, you also need to develop your inner temple—that is, prepare your mind and body for the practice of magic. As the inner temple develops, the importance of the outer temple diminishes accordingly.

The inner temple

B ecoming a mage is all about being fit—in every sense of the word—so you need to get in shape. Creating a magical personality requires breaking old habits and forming new ones. These new habits help to build the inner temple of the true self.

PRAYER AND MEDITATION
Start your day with a period of prayer and meditation. In prayer, acknowledge all of your blessings and ask for the grace to help you achieve your heart's desire. Then focus on your principal means of achieving this goal—self-knowledge through meditation.

Seated on your temple chair in the pharaonic or Egyptian god posture—feet

Adopt the Egyptian god posture for meditation.

flat on floor, palms down on thighs, and back straight—close your eyes and observe your mind at work, following your thoughts with increasing detachment. Breathing deeply and rhythmically through the nose, place your attention in the solar plexus at the top of the breastbone, where your inner sun shines. Feel the warm light spreading through your body, relaxing, soothing, and vitalizing every cell. Do not be surprised if you find it hard to achieve a state of relaxation at first—for most people, it takes around six weeks of practice.

KEEPING A MAGICAL DIARY

Keeping a magical diary can help you achieve self-knowledge. A standard desktop year diary with at least half a page per day is ideal. That way, you will leave accusing blanks if you fail to keep it daily. Record even the most apparently mundane details, particularly your failures and shortcomings, but also your progress and anything you deem significant. Many mages write down their dreams every morning upon awaking.

Onions

CLEANSING

Just as you cleaned your outer temple, you must also purify yourself. A ritual shower before prayer and meditation is a good way to start your magical day. All spirits have a discerning sense of smell. They do not like garlic (angels no more than vampires) and onions, but they do like fine incense, so it is worthwhile to smell good.

Record your magical progress in a diary.

Daily exercises

To prepare your inner temple, you should establish a routine of daily exercises and rituals and adhere to them as rigorously as possible.

Scrying

Scrying, or divination, is a way of interacting with the conscious universe. Even the most basic forms of scrying, such as pendulum dowsing, can be extremely effective. Dowsers refer to the technique as "relaxed concentration." Pendulum dowsing can be performed with any weight attached to a piece of thread. Traditionally, a ring suspended from an 8-in. (20-cm) length of silk thread will do the trick.

1. *Sit at a table with a glass in front of you. Using the hand you write with, hold the pendulum between thumb and index finger. Prop your elbow on the table next to the glass and allow the pendulum to dangle directly in front of you on the other side of the glass.*

2. *Decide what question you are going to ask and to whom you will address it—for example, a guardian angel, an inner teacher, or a ghost. Establish the presence of your hidden ally by saying aloud:*

   "Will someone please answer my question?"

3. *You may answer by allowing the pendulum to knock against the glass—two knocks for a yes, one knock for a no. If you get one knock, you know you have a joker in your hand. If you get a positive response, go ahead and establish the identity of your respondent as closely as you can, then ask your question and wait for the answer.*

Scrying can be used to ask your guardian angel a question.

Developing second sight

1. Rub your palms together vigorously until they are charged with heat. Place your palms over your open eyes, blocking out the light. Relax and stare into the velvet blackness while feeling your eyes absorbing the warmth. When your palms have cooled, repeat the process.

2. Point your index fingers at each other a few inches in front of your open eyes. Bring the fingertips together and then separate them again. You should notice a double-nailed "sausage" finger appearing between them. Bring this disembodied finger into clear focus and hold it steady for a couple of minutes without straining. Palm your eyes as before.

3. The next day, try drawing two identical squares a couple of inches apart on a piece of paper. Hold the paper in front of your eyes and allow yourself to go slightly cross-eyed until a third shape appears in the middle. Hold your attention on the middle shape.

4. The day after, draw a pair of transparent cubes. See a third appear and float off the page. The greater the complexity of image that you can focus on, the more developed your second sight will become.

When experimenting with these exercises, be sure to palm your eyes as described in step 1 before and after each session. Do it for just a few minutes once or twice a day, taking care not to strain your eyes.

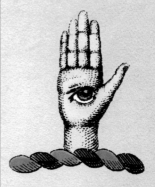

Palming helps to relax the eyes and prevent straining them.

Visualization exercises where you concentrate on images such as cubes help to focus the mind.

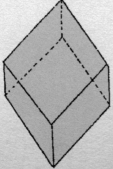

FIRE

Direction: South

Implement: Dagger

Color: Red

Function: Feeling

Sense: Sight

Metals: Iron, gold

Incense: Frankincense

Time: Noon

Season: Summer

Tetramorph: Lion

Divine name: Yahweh Tzabaoth (lord of hosts)

Archangel: Michael

Angel: Aral

Elemental: Salamander

Elemental king: Djin

Elemental ruler: Seraph

AIR

Direction: East

Implement: Wand

Color: Yellow

Function: Thinking

Sense: Hearing

Metals: Mercury, quicksilver

Incense: Galbanum

Time: Dawn

Season: Spring

Tetramorph: Man

Divine name: Shaddai el Chai (almighty living god)

Archangel: Raphael

Angel: Chassan

Elemental: Sylph

Elemental king: Paralda

Elemental ruler: Ariel

The four elements—fire, air, water, and earth—represent the forces of nature that make up the material world of the cosmos. These are the mundane or physical elements that emerge from a source element known as spirit or quintessence.

The four

 Fire: *Fire is hot and dry. It is symbolized by an upward-pointing triangle, being volatile and ascending.*

 Air: *Air is hot and moist. Its triangle is crossed, putting a brake on the ascending nature of fire.*

 Water: *Water is cold and moist. As the descending element, its sign is a downward-pointing triangle.*

 Earth: *Earth is cold and dry. It halts the fall of water, so its triangle is crossed.*

Salamander, the elemental of fire.

elements

The four elements are not the common substances with which they share their names. They are principles, and these principles are paired with four qualities—hot, cold, dry, and moist. Each element shares one of its qualities with another element. This provides the dynamic that allows for transformation within matter. Earthy solids can melt into watery liquids, which in turn can become gases, and then condense back into fluid or burn. Fire is the most volatile of the elements; earth, the most fixed. Fire and air are the masculine elements, earth and water feminine. All things are mixtures of the four elemental qualities.

WATER

Direction: West
Implement: Cup
Colors: Black, blue
Function: Intuition
Sense: Taste
Metal: Silver
Incense: Myrrh
Time: Sunset
Season: Fall
Tetramorph: Eagle
Divine name: Elohim Tzabaoth (god of hosts)
Archangel: Gabriel
Angel: Taliahad
Elemental: Undine
Elemental king: Necksa
Elemental ruler: Tharsis

EARTH

Direction: North
Implement: Pantacle
Colors: White, black, brown
Function: Sensation
Sense: Touch
Metal: Lead
Incense: Storax
Time: Midnight
Season: Winter
Tetramorph: Ox
Divine name: Adonai ha Aretz (lord of the earth)
Archangel: Uriel
Angel: Phorlakh
Elemental: Gnome
Elemental king: Ghob
Elemental ruler: Kerub

One of the first tasks of the neophyte is to make the magical objects that represent the four elements—fire, air, water, and earth. These objects are used to implement the magical will and are the chief tools of the mage.

The magical implements

Naming the dagger

The dagger is the implement of fire and corresponds to the south, which the archangel Michael protects. The dagger represents strength, energy, courage, and will.

1. *If you cannot forge your own dagger, you may buy one, but be sure that it has not been used for magical purposes before. Unlike a knife, it should be equal-sided and double-edged. You will know your dagger when you find it—it will feel right in your hand.*

2. *Personalize your dagger by giving it a name. Choose the name with care, and make sure that it is free from ambivalent or negative connotations. The name may come to you during meditation or in a dream.*

3. *You can also engrave the Hebrew name of the archangel Michael on the blade.*

מיכאל Michael

Making the wand

1. Select a hardwood tree that will provide a straight stick that is ½–1 in. (1–2.5 cm) thick and 1–3 ft. (30–90 cm) long. Ash, hazel, elder, willow, birch, hawthorn, and blackthorn trees are all good choices.

2. Offer the tree a gift of tobacco or silver, and explain what you wish to do. Allow the tree a moment to withdraw its energy, then cut the branch with your dagger. Put some mud on the cut area to help heal the wound.

3. Trim off any side twigs or thorns, and carefully peel off the bark. Allow the wand to dry naturally for a couple of weeks.

4. Cut a 1-in. (2.5-cm) long notch into the narrower end of the wand using a fine saw blade. Rub the wand with sandpaper, and polish it with beeswax for a silky finish. Carefully inscribe the Hebrew name for the archangel Raphael along the wand.

5. Magnetize a length of piano wire by stroking a magnet along it in one direction. Tightly bind the wire around the notched end of the wand.

The wand is the implement of air, the realm of the rational mind and inspiration, and corresponds to the east. It comes under the lordship of the archangel Raphael.

רפאל

Raphael

When working with an element, insert an appropriate item into the notch on the wand—a feather for air, a shell for water, a stone for earth, or a match for fire.

Inscribing the cup

The cup used in magic is like a chalice or grail. It represents the soul, the element of water, and the west, whose guardian is the archangel Gabriel. Water is the primary passive element, just as fire is the primary active element. Water has a magnetic, attracting quality to it; like a cup, it receives and holds. It is psychic and intuitive and represents the archetypal feminine principle.

1. *The cup is traditionally made of silver or glass. Rather than buying a cup, it is best to receive it as a gift from someone who loves you unconditionally, like a parent or sibling.*

2. *Inscribe the cup with the Hebrew characters that spell the name of the archangel Gabriel.*

3. *A silver cup is relatively easy to inscribe with a sharp metal point, whereas a glass cup must be engraved with a special glass-engraving tool. In a pinch, you can paint the name with blue enamel paint.*

Gabriel

גבריאל

Pentagram

Hexagram

Making the pantacle

1. *You will need a solid disk of wood, stone, clay, or animal horn, about 4 in. (10 cm) in diameter. Leaving a 1-in. (2.5-cm) border around the outside of the disk, inscribe a hexagram—the six-pointed seal of Solomon—onto one side. This represents the macrocosm, the godhead.*

2. *Inscribe a pentagram—the five-pointed star—on the other side. This represents a human being with spread legs and outstretched arms and symbolizes the microcosm, man as the image of God. The pantacle therefore represents the mage in relationship with the divine.*

3. *On the border of the macrocosm side, inscribe the Hebrew characters for the archangel Uriel.*

The pantacle usually has a pentagram on one side. As a result, it is often misnamed pentacle, a synonym for pentangle or pentagram. Pentacle means five angles, being a five-pointed star. The pantacle, however, means all angles, being a disk shaped like a solid wheel. The pantacle is the magical implement of the element earth. It represents the body, the most material factor of life, and corresponds to the north, which the archangel Uriel defends.

וריאל Uriel

Consecrating the implements

Consecrating the magical implements is a complicated process
and incorporates various rituals described elsewhere in this
book—the kabbalistic cross of light (see page 90) and the
rituals of the pentagram (see pages 64–67). You will also
need to make some holy water (see page 57).

The consecration rite

The general rite is
described here. You
need to use the specified
time, direction, color,
pentagram, and invocations
for the individual implement
that you are consecrating.

1. At the appropriate time for the implement that you
   are consecrating, place some burning incense and
   a glass of holy water on the altar, then put items in
   the appropriate quarter of the altar to represent the
   four elements.

   North: *A pinch of salt on some bread to denote earth.*
   South: *A lit candle or oil lamp to represent fire.*
   East: *A rose or some dried rose petals to symbolize air.*
   West: *A cup of red wine or grape juice to signify water.*

2. Perform the kabbalistic cross of light and the lesser
   banishing ritual of the pentagram.

3. Pick up the glass of holy water, and sprinkle some into
   the four quarters while walking clockwise around the
   temple. Walk the circle again, this time with the incense.
   Walk the circle three more times, pausing in the east
   each time to say:

   "Holy, holy, holy, creator of the universe.
   Holy, holy, holy, formless lord of life.
   Holy, holy, holy, the absolute almighty,
   Master of polarity, lord of dark and light."

4. *Perform the greater invoking ritual of the pentagram.*

5. *Facing the direction associated with the tool, and with the altar in front of you, trace the appropriate invoking pentagram over the implement. Recite the first invocation, resonating the names.*

Dagger: First invocation
"In the holy and divine name of Yahweh Tzabaoth (pronounced Yah-way Tza-bah-oth), whose fire and light is the spark of all life, I invoke you great archangel Michael (Mee-kay-el), lord of fire. I entreat you to preside over this rite of consecration. May your angel Aral (Ah-ral) guide my steps upon the path. May the mighty prince Seraph (Seh-raf), ruler of fire, with the blessing of the almighty, invest this dagger with the sacred powers and virtues whereby I may perform the operations for which it is designed."

Wand: First invocation
"In the holy and divine name of Shaddai el Chai (pronounced Shah-dye el Hai), whose word is the breath of all life, I invoke you great archangel Raphael (Rah-fay-el), lord of air. I entreat you to preside over this rite of consecration. May your angel Chassan (Chah-san) guide my steps upon the path. May the mighty prince Ariel (Ah-ree-el), ruler of air, with the blessing of the almighty, invest this wand with the sacred powers and virtues whereby I may perform the operations for which it is designed."

TIME AND DIRECTION

Dagger
Consecrate the dagger at summer solstice if possible. Face south when reciting the invocations.

Wand
Ideally, the rite should take place at fall equinox. Face east when reciting the invocations.

Cup
Spring equinox is the best time to perform this rite. Face west when reciting the invocations.

Pantacle
Consecrate the pantacle at winter solstice. Face north when reciting the invocations.

Dagger
Fire-invoking pentagram

Wand
Air-invoking pentagram

Cup
Water-invoking pentagram

Pantacle
Earth-invoking pentagram

Each invocation calls upon the assistance of angels and spirits connected with the implement's associated element.

Cup: First invocation

"In the holy and divine name of Elohim Tzabaoth (pronounced El-oh-heem Tza-bah-oth), whose celestial waters bore all the forms of creation, I invoke you great archangel Gabriel (Gah-bree-el), lord of water. I entreat you to preside over this rite of consecration. May your angel Taliahad (Tah-lee-ah-had) guide my steps upon the path. May the mighty prince Tharsis (Thah-sis), ruler of water, with the blessing of the almighty, invest this cup with the sacred powers and virtues whereby I may perform the operations for which it is designed."

Pantacle: First invocation

"In the holy and divine name of Adonai ha Aretz (pronounced Ah-don-ai ha Ah-retz), who did create humankind as the salt of the earth, I invoke you great archangel Uriel (Oo-ree-el), lord of earth. I entreat you to preside over this rite of consecration. May your angel Phorlakh (For-lac) guide my steps upon the path. May the mighty prince Kerub (Kee-rub), ruler of earth, with the blessing of the almighty, invest this pantacle with the sacred powers and virtues whereby I may perform the operations for which it is designed."

6. *Trace the appropriate invoking pentagram over the implement once again (see page 29). Recite the second invocation, resonating the names. Use the tool to trace the invoking pentagram in each quarter.*

Dagger: Second invocation

"In the name of Yahweh Tzabaoth (pronounced Yah-way Tza-bah-oth) and of the great archangel Michael (Mee-kay-el), his angel Aral (Ah-ral), and the mighty prince Seraph (Seh-raf), ruler of fire, I do command the elemental spirits of fire to recognize and obey the power invested in this dagger and the authority of the one who wields it, that they may take delight in assisting all its operations."

Wand: Second invocation

"In the name of Shaddai el Chai (pronounced Shah-dye el Hai), and of the great archangel Raphael (Rah-fay-el), his angel Chassan (Chah-san), and the mighty prince Ariel (Ah-ree-el), ruler of air, I do command the elemental spirits of air to recognize and obey the power invested in this wand and the authority of the one who wields it, that they may take delight in assisting all its operations."

Cup: Second invocation

"In the name of Elohim Tzabaoth (pronounced El-oh-heem Tza-bah-oth), and of the great archangel Gabriel (Gah-bree-el), his angel Taliahad (Tah-lee-ah-had), and the mighty prince Tharsis (Thah-sis), ruler of water, I do command the elemental spirits of water to recognize and obey the power invested in this cup and the authority of the one who wields it, that they may take delight in assisting all its operations."

Pantacle: Second invocation

"In the name of Adonai ha Aretz (pronounced Ah-don-ai ha Ah-retz), and of the great archangel Uriel (Oo-ree-el), his angel Phorlakh (For-lac), and the mighty prince Kerub (Kee-rub), ruler of earth, I do command the elemental spirits of earth to recognize and obey the power invested in this pantacle and the authority of the one who wields it, that they may take delight in assisting all its operations."

7. Perform the kabbalistic cross of light. Wrap the implement in a piece of silk of the appropriate color.

8. Repeat step 3, but this time walk counterclockwise and make the same recitation in the west. Remain in the west and say:

   "Any spirits caught in the circle I now set free in the name of peace."

9. Perform the lesser banishing ritual of the pentagram.

COLORS

Dagger
White or red silk.

Wand
White or yellow silk.

Cup
White, black, or blue silk.

Pantacle
White, black, or brown silk.

Holy water is used to purify and consecrate the implements.

The Three Pillars of High Magic

The three pillars of the hermetic arts and sciences that underpin the practice of high magic are astrology (the influence of the planets and stars), alchemy (the preparation of magical elixirs), and magic (key rituals for engaging elemental and cosmic forces based around sacred figures such as the pentagram and hexagram).

The hermetic dictum "as above, so below" is nowhere more clearly exemplified than in astrology. The planets of the solar system and the constellations of the zodiac have long been known to bring influences to bear here on Earth. All things in the universe are woven into the intricate patterns of the cosmic loom and the endless dance of the planets and the stars.

The seven lords

It is no wonder that the ancient Greeks, Romans, and other civilizations conceived of the planets as gods. After all, they have particular qualities that are like those used to describe personalities. Words such as mercurial (Mercury), saturnine (Saturn), jovial (Jupiter), and lunatic (Moon) were all used to define the attributes of the planetary gods and are still in use today to describe the same character traits. The qualities and virtues of the planets also correspond directly to the sephiroth of the kabbalistic tree of life (see pages 80–91).

Celestial gods of the ancient Greeks and Romans.

The twelve signs of the zodiac are based on the twelve constellations of stars through which the planets rotate throughout the year. Each zodiac sign has its own distinctive attributes and influences.

ACHIEVING HARMONY

The planets must be considered not merely in isolation, but also in relationship with each other. The relationship of the planets—their mutual position in space at the moment we are born—has a great bearing on our predispositions as individuals. Although there is not sufficient space in this book to give more than an outline of the planets' attributes and correspondences, it should be clear that the study of astrology forms one of the principle pillars of high magic.

By understanding the astrological predispositions within yourself, you can make a conscious effort to become free from constrictive or unbalanced behavior patterns and achieve harmonious resonance with all the planetary spheres.

As the planets change position within the zodiac, they bring different influences to bear here on Earth.

ħ *Planetary symbol for Saturn.*

Cronus

Saturn

Guardian of the threshold

✳

Saturn is the guardian of the threshold between the material and the spiritual worlds, the gateway between eternity and the realm of time and space. The most distant and slowest moving of the visible planets, Saturn is where the descent into matter begins. It is the planet of restriction and inhibition. As the lord of order, self-knowledge, and discipline, Saturn can be a severe taskmaster. It governs all condensing, crystallizing, and hardening processes, ruling the skeleton and aging. Saturn is equated to the skeletal figure of Death or Old Father Time, cutting down the old, useless, or unworthy with his scythe.

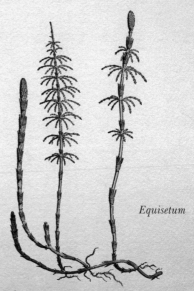

Equisetum

CORRESPONDENCES

Principles: Inhibition, concentration
Element: Earth
Colors: Iridescent black, purple
Day: Saturday
Polarity: Yin
Zodiac signs: Capricorn, Aquarius
Numbers: 3, 32
Tarot cards: The World, the threes
Sephirah: Binah (understanding)
Chakra: Muladhara (feet)
Metal: Lead
Alchemical process: Calcination
Deities: Cronus/Saturn, Ceridwen, Kali
Archangel: Cassiel
Angel: Oriphiel
Planetary intelligence: Agiel
Planetary spirit: Zazel
Creatures: Tortoise, beaver, vole, crow, ant, termite
Stones: Onyx, jet, diamond, obsidian, black coral
Incense: Myrrh, spikenard, harmal, copal, aloe
Trees: Beech, holly, poplar, Scotch pine, yew
Healing plants: Equisetum, comfrey, heartsease, red root, uva ursi
Body parts: Bone structure, teeth, tendons, joints, spleen
Body functions: All hardening and aging processes
Mental function: Long-term memory
Malfunctions: Rheumatism, depression, lethargy, aging
Virtues: Discipline, sincerity, humility, perseverance, acceptance, wisdom
Vices: Melancholy, crankiness, distrust, isolation, inflexibility, meanness
Keyword: Saturnine

Capricorn

Symbolism

- *In alchemy, Saturn represents the process of calcination, when impurities are burned off in the purifying fire.*
- *The terrifying Kali aspect of Saturn can precipitate the nadir, the terrible turmoil that ends only when we abandon vanity and falseness and commit to the path of return.*
- *The payoff for surviving this ordeal is the energizing of the base chakra, Muladhara, and the awakening of Kundalini, the serpent power coiled at the base of the spine. The person then becomes an initiate through accomplishing this first stage of the great work.*

Tortoise

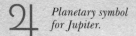

24 *Planetary symbol for Jupiter.*

Jupiter
The joybringer

Jupiter is by far the largest of the visible planets. It has thirteen moons, attracted by its powerful magnetic field. Its energies are carried to Earth by the solar wind. In contrast to the restrictive and inhibitory qualities of Saturn, Jupiter is expansive, generous, warm, and jovial. He is the fire of nature, the warmth in all things. In mythology, he is the lusty, self-indulgent king of the Olympian gods. This tendency to excess is Jupiter's main weakness, and in physical terms can lead to liver problems. Besides controlling the liver, Jupiter also rules the immune system. Jupiter presides over harmony, law, and religion.

Jove

Borage

CORRESPONDENCES

Principles: Harmony, justice

Elements: Fire, air

Colors: Mauve, blue, purple, gray

Day: Thursday

Polarity: Yang

Zodiac signs: Sagittarius, Pisces

Numbers: 4, 21

Tarot cards: The Wheel of Fortune, the fours

Sephirah: Chesed (mercy)

Chakra: None

Metals: Tin, zinc

Alchemical processes: Sublimation, distillation

Deities: Zeus/Jupiter/Jove, Sobek, Math, Dagda

Archangel: Tzadkiel

Angel: Sachiel

Planetary intelligence: Yophiel

Planetary spirit: Hismael

Creatures: Whale, dolphin, fish, elephant, horse, eagle, water birds, bee

Stones: Sapphire, lapis lazuli, amethyst, turquoise, tanzanite

Incense: Myrrh, sandalwood, benzoin, gum mastic, cedar, fennel, nutmeg

Trees: Oak, ash, maple, horse chestnut, cedar

Healing plants: Arnica, borage, lemon balm, sage, ginseng, comfrey, echinacea

Body parts: Liver, arteries, digestive organs, buttocks, right ear, outer sex organs, feet

Body functions: Immune system, sugar economy, energy conservation, cell formation, food assimilation

Mental functions: Memory, humor

Malfunctions: Cancer, cirrhosis, stomach ulcer

Virtues: Generosity, fairness, benevolence, mercy, compassion

Vices: Vanity, self-indulgence, greediness, materialism

Keyword: Jovial

Sagittarius

Symbolism

- *Jupiter rules the alchemical processes of sublimation and distillation, which in nature produce dew—moisture that is refined as it is drawn from the earth and that absorbs cosmic energy as it recondenses.*

- *Sublimation is symbolized by Jupiter, in the form of an eagle, carrying his cup-bearer Ganymede to heaven.*

- *Jupiter's seduction of Danae, the daughter of the king of Argos, in the form of a golden shower symbolizes the distillation of philosophical gold.*

Eagle

Planetary symbol for Mars.

Mars
The warrior

✸

The fiery red planet represents the intensely masculine, active, dynamic principle of life. Its effects are intensifying, accelerating, and violent. As the god of war, Mars has a reputation, along with Saturn, as a malign body at conflict with the other planets. The negative aspects of Mars include ruthlessness, destruction, and brutality. The positive aspects of Mars are determination, willpower, courage, and passion. Mars rules the muscular system, sex organs, and blood formation.

Ares

Nettle

CORRESPONDENCES

Principle: Force

Element: Fire

Color: Red

Day: Tuesday

Polarity: Yang

Zodiac signs: Aries, Scorpio

Numbers: 5, 27

Tarot cards: The Tower, the fives

Sephirah: Geburah (strength, severity)

Chakra: Svadhistthana (genitals)

Metal: Iron

Alchemical process: Separation

Deities: Ares/Mars, Tiu/Tyr, Bishamon, Nergal, all war gods

Archangel: Camael

Angel: Zamael

Planetary intelligence: Nakhiel

Planetary spirit: Bartzabel

Creatures: Horse, fox, ram, robin, scorpion, all stinging insects other than bees

Stones: Ruby, garnet, bloodstone, carnelian

Incense: Cyprus, aloe, tobacco, pine, red cedar

Trees: Thorn, pine, savin, cyprus, rhododendron

Healing plants: Hawthorn, nettle, sarsaparilla, vomic nut, basil

Body parts: Muscular system, red corpuscles, sex organs, gall, astral body

Body functions: Body heat, blood formation

Mental function: Engagement

Malfunctions: Fever, inflammation, high blood pressure, hemorrhage

Virtues: Courage, determination, passion, protection

Vices: Wrath, impulsiveness, ruthlessness, brutality, destructiveness

Keyword: Martial

Scorpio

Symbolism

- *Mars governs the polarity between the brain and sexual organs. This is the conduit for Kundalini, the serpent power in Indian yoga.*
- *Mars is associated with the alchemical process of separation, which can be brutal and painful.*
- *Known as the iron planet, the uses of its metal reflect strength and aggression—swords, guns, armor, engines.*
- *Camael, its archangel, is a powerful protector and guide, providing courage and determination.*

Ram

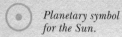

Planetary symbol for the Sun.

Sun

Lord of light

The Sun is the radiant heart of the solar system, without which there could be no life. The Sun is vitality, the will to live, consciousness, and spirit. As a planetary sphere, the Sun's influence is benign, but if overemphasized it can engender pride and self-centeredness. Without the cooling, moistening influence of the Moon, it can be harsh, arid, and burning. The Sun rules the individual mind, energy, and willpower. Physiologically, it governs the heart, circulation, and health.

Apollo

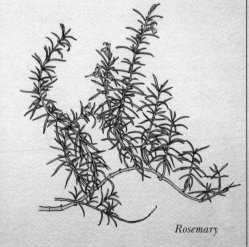

Rosemary

CORRESPONDENCES

Leo

Principles: Consciousness, vitality

Element: Fire

Colors: Gold, red

Day: Sunday

Polarity: Yang

Zodiac sign: Leo

Numbers: 6, 30

Tarot cards: The Sun, the sixes

Sephirah: Tiphareth (beauty)

Chakra: Anahata (heart)

Metal: Gold

Alchemical processes: Coagulation, conjunction

Deities: Apollo, Helios, Bel, Ra, Mithras

Archangel: Michael

Angel: Raphael

Planetary intelligence: Nakhiel

Planetary spirit: Sorath

Creatures: Lion, all cats, blackbird, yellow and orange butterflies

Stones: Ruby, tiger's eye, amber, chrysolite

Incense: Frankincense, myrrh, copal, cinnamon, bergamot

Trees: Walnut, ash, citrus, laurel, juniper

Healing plants: Chamomile, cinnamon, clove, eyebright, ginger, St. John's wort, rosemary

Body parts: Heart, spine, solar plexus, eyes

Body functions: Circulation, heat and energy distribution

Malfunctions: Low vitality, cardiac problems

Virtues: Health, vitality, organization, power

Vices: Pride, egotism

Keyword: Solar

Symbolism

- *The Sun is equated with gold, the ideal metal, which it evolves to perfection by its heat and transforming rays in the crucible of the Earth.*

- *The Sun is a manifestation of the divine light in the kabbalistic realm of Yetzirah, the world of formation.*

- *As the celestial consort of the Moon, the Sun is the masculine principle, the active, engendering seed that alchemists refer to as the father of the stone.*

- *Appropriately, the Sun's corresponding chakra is Anahata, the heart chakra.*

Cat

Planetary symbol
for Venus.

Venus

Goddess of love

Venus is the planet of affectionate love, the muse of art, friendship, and music. As the ruler of Libra, Venus helps to mediate between opposites and to integrate diverse elements into harmonious balance. Like Mercury, Venus is a great mediator, being the muse of relating. Venus rules important organs and functions within the human body, including the kidneys, inner sexual organs, blood and cell formation, and the sense of smell. An exaggeration of the Venusian principle is associated with wantonness and venereal disease.

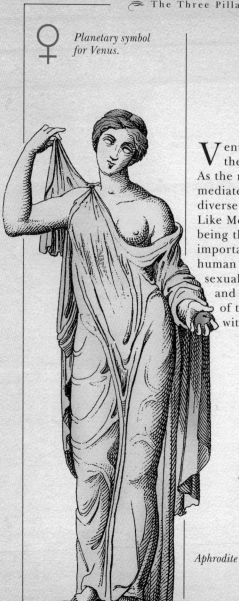

Aphrodite

Apple

CORRESPONDENCES

Principles: Relating, art

Element: Air

Colors: Rose, emerald

Day: Friday

Polarity: Yin

Zodiac signs: Libra, Taurus

Numbers: 7, 14

Tarot cards: The Empress, the sevens

Sephirah: Netzach (victory)

Chakra: Vissudha (throat)

Metal: Copper

Alchemical process: Fermentation

Deities: Aphrodite/Venus, Sukra, Ishtar, Benten, Lakshmi, Chenrezi

Archangel: Haniel

Angel: Anael

Planetary intelligence: Hagiel

Planetary spirit: Kedemel

Creatures: Deer, rabbit, dove, swallow, butterfly

Stones: Emerald, rose quartz, opal, jade, malachite, pink coral

Incense: Sandalwood, storax, galbanum, valerian, violet, rose

Trees: Apple, pear, cherry, elder, linden, chestnut

Healing plants: Yarrow, lady's mantle, motherwort, vervain

Body parts: Complexion, upper lip, throat, breasts, kidneys, abdomen, inner sexual organs

Body functions: Cell and nerve formation, diuretic and emetic processes, sense of smell

Malfunctions: Problems relating to sexual organs and kidneys

Virtues: Harmony, proportion, beauty, affection

Vices: Sentimentality, immodesty, tastelessness, sexual intemperance

Keyword: Relating

Taurus

Symbolism

- *Venus is commonly viewed as the goddess of love, known as Aphrodite to the ancient Greeks, but to the Indians this planetary deity is the masculine Sukra.*
- *Venus is associated with the alchemical process of fermentation. Legend relates that Sukra possessed the elixir of immortality, known in western alchemy as the white lion or white stone.*
- *The metal of Venus is copper, which is highly conductive.*
- *The offspring of the deities Venus and Mercury is the divine hermaphrodite, the adept who has achieved active equilibrium.*

Deer

*Planetary symbol
for Mercury.*

Hermes

Mercury
The cosmic messenger

Mercury is the fastest moving planet, the quicksilver messenger service mediating between above and below. It rules mental processes, travel, communication, language, writing, adaptability, and the intellect. To the Romans, Mercury was the god of both merchants and thieves. The planet has a cool, ambivalent, unreliable quality akin to the trickster figure, who sets pitfalls for people in order to reveal their foolishness and keep them on the right path. There is a puckish, teasing tendency that exposes falsehood and conceit. As a planetary entity, Mercury is androgynous, containing all opposites within himself. He is therefore a free operator, independent of a polar opposite, although he does have an antagonistic relationship with Saturn.

Lavender

CORRESPONDENCES

Virgo

Principles: Mediation, intelligence

Element: Air

Colors: Orange, yellow

Day: Wednesday

Polarity: Yin/yang

Zodiac signs: Gemini, Virgo

Numbers: 8, 12

Tarot cards: The Magician, the eights

Sephirah: Hod (glory)

Chakra: Sahasrara (crown of head)

Metal: Quicksilver

Alchemical processes: Circulation, mediation

Deities: Hermes/Mercury, Thoth, Quetzalcoatl, Viracocha, Kukulkan

Archangel: Raphael

Angel: Michael

Planetary intelligence: Tiriel

Planetary spirit: Taphthartharath

Creatures: Coyote, monkey, raven, ibis, fly

Stones: Opal, topaz, tourmaline, carnelian, peridot

Incense: Anise, lavender, gum arabic, storax

Trees: Hazel, acacia, myrtle, mulberry

Healing plants: Wormwood, digitalis, mandrake, valerian, skullcap, parsley, caraway

Body parts: Ears, tongue, nervous system, hands, feet, lungs, spinal cord, thyroid

Body functions: Mental and nervous processes, hearing, speech, respiration, coordination

Malfunctions: Impairment of nerves and motor functions, speech impediments, dyslexia

Virtues: Communication, mediation, sound judgment, diplomacy

Vices: Trickery, coldness, stinginess, mental cruelty

Keyword: Mercurial

Symbolism

- In alchemy, Mercury plays distracting tricks, forcing the mage to pay close attention.
- Mercury's relationship with Saturn is symbolized alchemically by a child (Mercury) killing a dragon (Saturn), initiating the great work by dispatching the forces that imprison the prime matter of the soul.
- Mercury is associated with Sahasrara, the crown chakra, which exists in potential only. Sahasrara is only activated when the mage has achieved transcendental cosmic consciousness.

Raven

*Planetary symbol
for the Moon.*

Moon

Queen of the deep

✷

The Moon rules the emotions, instincts, and the subconscious. It is feminine, nurturing, reflective, and changeable. It influences fertility, growth, and conception. It also influences the waters of the oceans, the sap in plants, and all bodily fluids, as witnessed by the tides and the menstrual cycle of women. Everything that grows on the Earth does so in rhythm with the Moon. It rules dreams, intuition, and the way we feel. Its dark side is the unconscious and the wilder, baser instincts. Physiologically, it governs the stomach, cerebellum, and pancreas.

Diana

Poppy

CORRESPONDENCES

Principles: Psyche, emotion

Element: Water

Colors: Silver, violet, royal purple

Day: Monday

Polarity: Yin

Zodiac sign: Cancer

Numbers: 9, 13

Tarot cards: The High Priestess, the nines

Sephirah: Yesod (foundation)

Chakra: Ajna (between the eyes)

Metal: Silver

Alchemical processes: Conjunction, coagulation

Deities: Artemis/Diana, Isis, Selene, Cybele, Arianrhod, Astarte

Archangel: Gabriel

Angel: Gabriel

Planetary intelligence: Malkah Be

Planetary spirit: Chasmodai

Creatures: Shellfish, wolf, owl, nightingale, nightjar, moth, spider

Stones: Moonstone, pearl, aquamarine

Incense: Camphor, jasmine, ylang-ylang

Trees: Willow, magnolia

Healing plants: Chaste tree, cleaver, opium poppy, periwinkle, watercress

Body parts: Brain, womb, bladder, stomach, pancreas, body fluids

Body functions: Menstruation, growth, fertility, glandular secretion

Mental functions: Memory, subconscious, instinct, intuition, reflection, dreaming

Malfunctions: Psychosis, schizophrenia, lycanthropy

Virtues: Sensitivity, motherliness, benevolence

Vices: Moodiness, impressionability, hypersensitivity, defensiveness, envy

Keyword: Feeling

Cancer

Symbolism

- *The Moon corresponds to Ajna, the chakra that represents the third eye, the pineal gland located behind the area between the eyebrows.*
- *In alchemy, the Moon is often called Luna or Diana, the lunar goddess of the Greeks, and corresponds to the white lion, the white tincture that is the elixir of immortality.*
- *In polarity with its cosmic consort the Sun, the Moon is cold, moist, and passive, the feminine principle that receives the seed of sulfur and bears the hermaphroditic child.*

Wolf

The mage uses alchemy to prepare magical elixirs, such as planetary tinctures and fluid condensers. The practice of alchemy is a crucial part of the great work, and is also grounding and purifying.

Alchemy

Seventeenth-century illustration depicting the tria prima—anima (soul), spiritus (spirit), and corpus (body)— and the alchemical processes that will ultimately lead to the philosopher's stone.

Alchemy focuses on identifying and purifying the tria prima, the three principles of soul, spirit, and body—represented by sulfur, mercury, and salt, respectively. The processes used in the preparation of alchemical substances are symbolic of the inner purification of the mage. The search for the elusive philosopher's stone, which is said both to transmute base metals into gold and to be the elixir of immortality, signifies the alchemist's goal of achieving union with the divine. A great alchemical maxim is "solve et coagula," meaning "dissolve the body and coagulate the spirit." The alchemist liberates (dissolves) the secret fire contained within all physical materials, thereby purifying and spiritualizing (coagulating) them.

HEAVENLY DEW

To the alchemist, dew is the precipitation of the cosmic fire and a key solvent used in the purification processes of the tria prima. No other substance in nature more perfectly reflects the central alchemical process of circulation than dew. It is drawn up as moisture from the land by the action of the Sun and condensed by the cool of the night to settle again on the earth. It is the distilled essence of heaven above and earth below, a condensation of the universal spirit, known as prana in yoga and chi or qi in China. In the Kabbalah, dew represents resurrection.

The Mutus Liber

Many important alchemical elixirs and processes use dew. Dew features as the prima materia (prime material) in one of the most famous and influential alchemical books, the *Mutus Liber* (Mute Book), first published in 1677. Almost entirely wordless (hence the title), the book consists of fifteen engravings depicting a sequence of alchemical processes performed by a man and a woman.

*"I am the moisture that preserves
everything in nature and makes it live,
I pass from the upper to the lower planes;
I am the heavenly dew and the fat of the land;
I am the fiery water and the watery fire;
nothing may live without me…"*

**From *Secret Symbols of the Rosicrucians*, 1785,
a compendium of alchemical and mystical wisdom.**

Planetary tinctures

Plant alchemy, while known as the lesser work, is an important initiation in the scheme of the great work. The preparation of planetary tinctures liberates, purifies, and recombines in an exalted form the three principles in plants: the soul/sulfur, or the essential oil; the spirit/mercury, or the plant alcohol (hence spirit); and the body/salt, or the alkaline, water-soluble salts. Planetary tinctures have an extraordinary effect on every aspect of the mage's constitution.

Stage 1: Extracting sal salis

The first stage in creating a planetary tincture is to extract some water-soluble salts from plant matter. Sal salis means "salt of the salt" and is prepared from wood ashes. Hardwood is best because it contains less tar and resin. Ash (*Fraxinus*) and lime (*Tilia*) trees have the advantage of being ready to burn when freshly cut. Another consideration may be the planetary rulership of the source tree (see pages 36–49).

1. Lay a fire using untreated hardwood. The most efficient way to do this is in an open fireplace using a grate, but an outside fire ritual in a sacred spot during one of the solar or fire festivals, such as winter solstice or Imbolc, can produce a potent ash. Do not use paper because it usually contains undesirable materials. Use dry grass and twigs as kindling—never use prefabricated fire lighters. It is best to carry out this procedure on a sunny day so that you can use the Sun to ignite the fire. This is because the true nature of fire is to be found less in the fuel than in the agent of ignition. Fuel feeds a fire but is not its source.

2. Use a magnifying glass to focus the Sun's rays onto the wick of a candle until it becomes a flame. If the sunlight is weak, dip some filter paper in ethanol. The paper will readily catch fire, and you can use it to light the candle. Use the candle to light the fire you have laid, taking care to drip as little wax into the fire as possible. A high grate will allow you to light the fire from underneath and avoid dripping wax.

3. Keep adding fuel to the fire until it has produced 2½ gallons (10 liters) of ash (enough to fill a standard mop bucket).

4. Collect the ashes and grind any solid pieces to powder. Roast the ashes in a flameproof ceramic pot on top of a hot stove until they have turned gray. This heating process is known as calcination.

5. Allow the ashes to cool, then put them in a large enamel pan and add several gallons of filtered rainwater or spring water. Unless you have a huge pan, you will have to do this in several batches.

6. Boil the liquid ashes for about 15 minutes, then filter (through an unbleached coffee filter or filter paper) into another large enamel pan. The remaining solid matter is known as the caput mortuum (death head). Reserve a small amount for making holy water (see page 57), then return the rest to the earth.

7. Boil the filtered liquid, uncovered. As the liquid reduces, the salts will start to become visible. When nearly all the liquid has evaporated, the salts will start to sputter, so take care. Reduce the heat and, wearing gloves and goggles if necessary, stir the solidifying salts vigorously until they have hardened.

8. Break the salts into small pieces, drive off any remaining moisture in the oven, then calcine again over a high heat (covered) for at least an hour.

9. Dissolve the salts in filtered rainwater or spring water, then filter and evaporate again. Repeat this process until no residue is left in the filter. When finished, powder the pure, dry salts and place in an airtight jar. Keep a small amount in a separate container for making holy water.

EMOTIONAL RELEASE

Tending the fire to produce the required amount of ash in step 3 may take a long time, but the longer you can stay with the fire, giving it your full attention, the better. Take the opportunity to unburden your soul of any combustible old matter. Allow the heat of the fire to melt any stones in your heart. Let the emotion flow out of you and vaporize in the flames. Be aware of the spirits delighting in the fire.

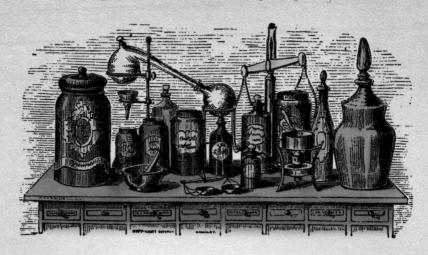

Stage 2: Producing the oleum salis

The alkaline salts extracted from the ashes in the form of sal salis are strongly hygroscopic—that is, they readily absorb moisture from the air. The alchemist uses these as a magnet for attracting dew. Once saturated with dew, the salts dissolve and become liquid, producing oleum salis (oil of salt).

1. *On a still, clear evening, ideally when the Sun is in Aries or Taurus, spread the sal salis about ½ in. (1 cm) deep in glass, glazed earthenware, or enamel dishes. Place the dishes in the open air about 1 ft. (30 cm) above the ground.*

2. *Retrieve the dishes before sunrise and check whether the salts have liquefied. If they have not, repeat the process the following night and again, if necessary.*

3. *Once the salts have liquefied, filter and preserve the liquid in a sealed bottle. This is the oleum salis, which provides the best solvent for extracting the planetary virtues from plants when creating planetary tinctures.*

Stage 3: Creating the tincture

1. On the appropriate day, pour a seventh of the oleum salis into a glass jar. Add sufficient crushed plant to be well covered by the oil.

2. Place the glass jar in a warm, dark cupboard. A tincture made with alcohol or vinegar would take 2–3 weeks to produce, but the concentration of cosmic fire in the oleum salis is sufficiently potent to extract a red tincture within a day or two.

3. Filter the red oil, and add to it an equal amount of pure plant spirit (ethanol, not denatured alcohol). Immediately seal the jar. The red tincture and the alcohol do not mix; the alcohol will float on top.

4. Place the sealed jar in a warm, dark place, such as a linen closet or an incubator. The spirit above (the alcohol) will gradually draw up the spiritual properties of the plant and the oil below. The residual impurities in the red tincture will collect at the level where the two liquids meet. It takes 1–3 months for the process to be completed.

5. Pour off the alcohol, and preserve it in a tightly sealed dark glass bottle. This is the planetary tincture.

The tincture should be extracted from a plant governed by the relevant planet. It should be slowly dried and then crushed into small pieces by hand. Start making the tincture on the first day associated with the planet that occurs after a new moon. (For appropriate plants and days, see page 56.)

FINISHING THE TINCTURE

The amount of time the alchemical process in step 4 takes to complete depends on how warm the sealed jar has been kept—approximately 3 months at 65°F (18°C) and 1 month at 90°F (32°C). During this time, the spirit will absorb some of the color from below and the lower tincture will become paler.

USING THE TINCTURE

Take no more than 10 drops per day in a little wine or water, starting on the morning of the first planetary day during a waxing moon.

Marjoram is a suitable plant for a tincture of Mercury.

Plants and days

When looking for appropriate plants to make a planetary tincture (see page 55), consult a good plant guide to confirm appearance, habitat, and growing season. If you cannot harvest your own, purchase some from a reliable herbal supplier. (See pages 36–49 for additional plants.)

Make a Moon tincture using willow.

Saturn: *Saturday; horsetail (Equisetum arvense); take care to avoid the many poisonous plants ruled by Saturn.*

Jupiter: *Thursday; lemon balm (Melissa officinalis).*

Mars: *Tuesday; the flowers, young leaves, or berries of the hawthorn (Crataegus) or the dried root of the stinging nettle (Urtica dioica).*

Sun: *Sunday; rosemary (Rosmarinus officinalis).*

Venus: *Friday; motherwort (Leonurus cardiaca) or lady's mantle (Alchemilla)—the Latin name alchemilla means "little alchemist."*

Mercury: *Wednesday; skullcap (Scutellaria), caraway (Carum carvi), marjoram (Origanum majorana), or oregano (Origanum vulgare).*

Moon: *Monday; fresh cleavers (Galium aparine), the bark of the willow (Salix), or the berries of the chaste tree (Vitex agnus-castus).*

Holy water

1. Place a glass of spring water or filtered rainwater on your altar. Put some sal salis and caput mortuum (plant ashes left over from making sal salis) into small dishes on the altar.

2. Perform the lesser banishing ritual of the pentagram (see pages 64–65).

3. Face north with the altar before you and extend your right hand over the salt. Visualize the light of holy energy flowing from your palm into the salt and say:

   "May this fire-purified salt of the earth become a heavenly salt possessing the wisdom of creation. May it sustain my soul, spirit, and body and preserve them from corruption. May it nourish the earth and fortify my heart. Amen."

4. Extend your hand over the ash and, as light flows from your palm, say:

   "May this ash return to the eternal fount of living water. May it be a fertile earth. May it bring forth the tree of life. Amen."

5. Walk around the altar until you stand on its east side, facing west. Pour the salt and ashes into the water and say:

   "In the salt of eternal wisdom, in the water of preparation, in the ash whence the new earth springeth, be all things accomplished unto the age of the ages. Amen."

Holy water is made from sal salis (see pages 52–53) and is used in rites of consecration and purification (see pages 28–31 and 113–115). If kept carefully preserved in a glass bottle, it will not lose its power.

Fluid condensers

All liquids and metals have particular magnetic qualities. They are able to absorb and store energies and energy patterns from any source. The mage uses these qualities to make fluid condensers for use in magical operations. Fluid condensers can be solid, liquid, or gaseous—it is the energies they accumulate that are fluid, rather than the condensers themselves. The most useful kinds are the liquid and solid condensers.

Tincture of gold

The most important ingredient in any fluid condenser is gold, which to the alchemist is the most perfect substance that nature produces on earth. Gold can be added to any type of fluid condenser. Even minute amounts are useful, especially in liquid condensers.

You can use a piece of jewelry, such as a gold ring, to make this tincture.

1. Take a piece of gold, the purer the better, but even 9-carat gold will do. Heat it until it is red hot, then drop it into a bowl containing ten times its weight of filtered rainwater (thunder-rainwater is ideal, particularly if it has been collected in a nonmetal container before hitting the ground). The water will hiss and sputter furiously, so protect yourself from scalding.

2. Retrieve the gold with a glass implement, such as a heatproof glass cup or ladle, and repeat the process at least another six times.

3. By this time, the water will have become saturated with gold atoms from the contracting metal. Filter the liquid into a glass bottle, and preserve it for magical use. Seven or eight drops are sufficient to charge up to 3 oz. (85 g) of fluid condenser.

Elemental fluid condensers

1. *Place the powdered plant in a tall glass jar, and cover it with unadulterated grape brandy just before sunrise on the first appropriate day following a new moon:*

Fire: *Tuesday*
Air: *Wednesday*
Water: *Monday*
Earth: *Saturday*

2. *Seal the jar and place it in a warm, dark location for 28 days.*

3. *Filter the alcohol and pour it into a dark glass bottle, adding an appropriate amount of gold tincture (see opposite).*

4. *If you have some salts (sal salis; see pages 52–53) derived from a plant connected with the relevant element, then the addition of even a few grains will be even more empowering.*

Pumpkin

These are very useful for operations involving the elements. You will need 2 oz. (55 g) of dried, powdered plant for each element.

ELEMENTAL PLANTS

Fire: *Eucalyptus (Eucalyptus), feverfew (Chrysanthemum parthenium), garlic (Allium sativum), mistletoe (Viscum album), mustard (Brassica), stinging nettle (Urtica dioica), pepper (Piper nigrum), pot marigold (Calendula officinalis).*

Air: *Apple (Malus), bergamot (Citrus bergamia), fennel seed (Foeniculum vulgare), cherry leaves (Prunus), southernwood (Artemisia abrotanum), mint (Mentha), oregano (Origanum vulgare), hazel (Corylus).*

Water: *Lily of the valley (Convallaria majalis), water lily (Nymphaea), white lotus (Nymphaea lotus), pumpkinseed (Cucurbita pepo), tarragon (Artemisia dracunculus), blue flag (Acorus calamus).*

Earth: *Comfrey (Symphytum), lovage (Levisticum officinale), patchouli (Pogostemon cablin), bloodroot (Sanguinaria canadensis), Solomon's seal (Polygonatum), mullein (Verbascum), yew (Taxus).*

Planetary fluid condensers

Planetary fluid condensers can be used for any magical operations, such as charging a talisman or amulet, where you wish to emphasize the qualities of a particular planet or its corresponding sphere on the tree of life. Planetary fluid condensers are made in the same way as elemental ones (see page 59), using one or more of the plants listed here.

Saturn: *Saturday; the leaves of poplar (Populus), horsetail (Equisetum arvense), and comfrey (Symphytum); avoid comfrey root because it is too glutinous.*

Jupiter: *Thursday; sage (Salvia) and the leaves of the oak tree (Quercus).*

Mars: *Tuesday; untreated tobacco (Nicotiana tabacum) and stinging nettles (Urtica dioica).*

Sun: *Sunday; eyebright (Euphrasia officinalis), rosemary (Rosmarinus officinalis), cinnamon (Cinnamomum zeylanicum or C. loureiroi), and St. John's wort (Hypericum).*

Venus: *Friday; vervain (Verbena officinalis), yarrow (Achillea millefolium), or any of the mints (Mentha).*

Mercury: *Wednesday; the leaves of acacia (Acacia), valerian (Valeriana officinalis), and hazel (Corylus).*

Moon: *Monday; the skin of cucumbers (Cucumis sativus) and the leaves of the willow (Salix).*

Use poplar leaves to make a Saturn fluid condenser.

Metal filings are used to make solid universal fluid condensers.

Universal fluid condensers

Liquid universal fluid condenser
Simply mix equal amounts of each of the seven planetary condensers (see opposite), and then add a couple more drops of gold tincture (see page 58).

Solid universal fluid condenser
You will need one part each (in volume) of lead, tin, iron, gold, copper, brass, silver, and aloe resin; three parts of animal charcoal (meat cooked until it turns black will do); and seven parts of coal. Grind all the ingredients as finely as possible, using suitable files for the metals. Mix together thoroughly and store safely.

You can combine ingredients to make a universal fluid condenser, in liquid or solid form, that is even more powerful than the sum of its parts. The condenser can be used for consecrating magical implements and many other magical operations.

CHARGING MAGICAL TOOLS

Solid universal fluid condenser is especially useful in preparing magic mirrors (a mirror impregnated with charged substances, such as this condenser, and used for scrying) and can also be used to charge wands. Drill a hole through the length of the wand, or just 1–2 in. (2.5–5 cm) into each end, then fill with condenser and plug with resin or wax.

Charge a mirror with universal fluid condenser for use in scrying.

The ancients combined sacred geometry and numerology to generate magical figures that express the profoundest relationships of the microcosm and the macrocosm. These stars of the wise form the basis of the key rituals of high magic. They are used to open and close magical operations and to attract and dispel elemental or cosmic forces.

Stars of the wise

THE MAGIC CIRCLE

The circle is a symbolic shape that has been used for magical rituals since ancient times. The circumference of the circle has no beginning and no end, and so represents eternity. It also separates that which is within from that which is without. Circles are primarily used in rituals to keep out unwanted influences and to contain any power raised for magical working. The principle geometric shapes of the pentagram and hexagram are used in rituals of high magic within this protective circle.

The pentagram

The five-pointed star of the pentagram is the holy cross of the five elements: the four physical elements of fire, air, water, and earth, plus the fifth element known as spirit, quintessence, aethyr, or akasha.

T he quintessence is the unifying source of all elemental energy, the matrix that allows energy to emerge through the four material elements. The pentagram is therefore a symbol of the quintessence and also a geometric symbol of man as the microcosm—the image of God imbued with spirit; the perfected man as lord of the elements, who governs the elements by the authority of his will.

Pentagram rituals

The pentagram is the principle feature of rituals used to dispel or attract spiritual energies. The two main rituals are the lesser ritual of the pentagram and the greater ritual of the pentagram. Whereas the greater ritual is used for specific magical operations, the lesser ritual should be performed twice each day to help the process of self-initiation (see pages 116–119). It puts the aspirant in contact with the invisible elemental forces of nature and establishes a means of directing those forces according to will. It cleanses the aura of all lower elemental interference and infuses the mage with divine light. It also creates a circle of energy within which all magical operations should take place.

Spirit

Air

Water

Earth

Fire

The lesser ritual of the pentagram

There are two versions of the ritual—the lesser banishing ritual and the lesser invoking ritual. The banishing ritual should be performed at sunset (or before going to bed) as part of your daily routine and at the start of any magical operation to clear the temple of unhelpful energies. The invoking ritual should be performed at sunrise (or upon rising) and during operations to attract desirable energies.

Earth-invoking pentagram

Earth-banishing pentagram

1. Perform the kabbalistic cross of light (see page 90).

2. Facing east and with your arm outstretched, draw the earth-invoking pentagram with your wand or the earth-banishing pentagram with your dagger, depending on the ritual you are performing. While doing this, imagine that you are tracing a line of bright blue flame in front of you.

3. Now bring your hand up to your chest and thrust it out as if stabbing the center of the pentagram you have just drawn, resonating the divine name of God:

   "Yeh-hoh-wah."

4. Keeping your arm raised, turn to the south, tracing a quarter circle of blue flame as you do so. Now trace the invoking or banishing pentagram of earth again, then thrust your arm to the center of the pentagram, resonating the divine name of God:

   "Ah-don-eye."

5. Keeping your arm raised, turn to the west, tracing another quarter circle of blue flame. Again, trace the invoking or banishing pentagram of earth, then thrust to the center of the pentagram, resonating the divine name of God:

   "Eh-ee-yay."

6. Keeping your arm raised, turn to the north, tracing another quarter circle of blue flame. Now trace the invoking or banishing pentagram of earth for the final time. Again, thrust to the center of the pentagram, resonating the divine name of God:

   "Ah-goo-la."

7. *Keeping your arm raised, turn once more to the east, completing the circle of flame, which now surrounds you with the flaming stars at each cardinal point.*

8. *Open wide your arms in the form of a cross and say:*

"Before me Raphael
[visualize a great yellow light with a violet aura]
Behind me Gabriel
[visualize a great blue light with an orange aura]
On my right Michael
[visualize a great red light with a green aura]
On my left Uriel
[visualize a great green light with a red–brown aura]
About me flames the pentagram
[visualize the great circle of pentagrams around you]
Above me the father
[visualize a flaming hexagram—a six-pointed star of two interlocking triangles]
Below me the mother
[visualize another flaming hexagram]
Within me the eternal flame."

9. *Perform the kabbalistic cross of light in conclusion.*

Form a cross with your body during the invocation in step 8.

Use a wand for invoking rituals.

Use a dagger for banishing rituals.

TOOLS FOR THE RITUAL

Perform the banishing ritual with your dagger and the invoking ritual with your wand. If you do not have these at hand, use the sign of benediction (index and middle finger extended, the other fingers tucked into the palm and covered by the thumb).

Sign of benediction.

The greater ritual of the pentagram

Once you have used the lesser ritual of the pentagram to prepare your temple (see pages 64–65), you should conduct the greater ritual of the pentagram to invoke or banish the elements for magical operations such as consecrating magical implements (see pages 28–31). This ritual incorporates all the elemental pentagrams to create a more dynamic energy.

SPIRIT PENTAGRAMS

Below are the four pentagrams of spirit. The active spirit pentagrams are connected with the active elements of fire and air; the passive spirit pentagrams, with the passive elements of water and earth.

1. *Perform the kabbalistic cross of light (see page 90).*

2. *Facing east, trace the active-invoking or banishing pentagram of spirit, depending on the ritual you are performing. As you trace the pentagram, resonate the divine name of God: "**Eh-heh-yeh.**"*

3. *Make the active or passive sign of the portal, then trace the air-invoking or banishing pentagram, resonating the divine name of God: "**Yeh-hoh-wah.**" Make the sign of air by stretching both arms upward and outward, with the elbows bent at right angles, the hands bent back, and the palms upward as if supporting a weight.*

4. *Facing south, trace the active-invoking or banishing pentagram of spirit, resonating the divine name of God: "**Eh-heh-yeh.**"*

5. *Make the active or passive sign of the portal, then trace the fire-invoking or banishing pentagram, resonating the divine name of God: "**Eh-loh-heem.**" Make the sign of fire by raising the arms above the head and joining the hands so that the tips of the fingers and thumbs meet to form a triangle.*

6. *Facing west, trace the passive-invoking or banishing pentagram of spirit, resonating the divine name of God: "**Ah-goo-la.**"*

Active-invoking

Active-banishing

Passive-invoking

Passive-banishing

Air-invoking   **Fire-invoking**   **Water-invoking**   **Earth-invoking**

Air-banishing   **Fire-banishing**   **Water-banishing**   **Earth-banishing**

7. *Make the active or passive sign of the portal, then trace the water-invoking or banishing pentagram, resonating the divine name of God: "**El**." Make the sign of water by raising the arms until the elbows are level with the shoulders, then bring the hands across the chest, touching the thumbs and fingertips to form a triangle.*

8. *Facing north, trace the passive-invoking or banishing pentagram of spirit, resonating the divine name of God: "**Ah-goo-la**."*

9. *Make the active or passive sign of the portal, then trace the earth-invoking or banishing pentagram, resonating the divine name of God: "**Ah-don-eye**." Make the sign of earth by advancing the right foot, then stretch out the right hand upward and forward, the left hand downward and backward, and keep the palms open.*

10. *Turn once more to the east, completing the circle of flame, which now surrounds you with the flaming stars at each cardinal point.*

11. *Complete the ritual by repeating steps 8 and 9 of the lesser ritual of the pentagram.*

ELEMENT PENTAGRAMS

Above are the eight element pentagrams. Use the invoking pentagrams for the greater invoking ritual, and the banishing pentagrams for the greater banishing ritual.

SIGN OF THE PORTAL

Extend the arms, palms outward, in front of the body. Then separate the arms as if opening a curtain to invoke, or bring the palms together in a closing motion to banish.

The hexagram

The hexagram is a six-pointed star, made by interlocking two equilateral triangles. In hermetic science, it is known as the seal of Solomon. In legend, it was delivered to King Solomon by the archangel Raphael as the seal of a ring with which he might bind the demons that were disrupting the building of the temple.

The seal of Solomon—the hexagram—symbolizes the union of the macrocosm above and the microcosm below.

I n Indian alchemy, the hexagram is known as the sri yantra, being the complete interpenetration of Shiva and Shakti, male and female, respectively. The mystic alchemist Jacob Boehme called it "the most meaningful sign in the entire universe." He saw it as a symbol of Christ as androgyne, the perfectly balanced, all-reconciling divine human.

DIVINE UNION
The interlocking triangles of the hexagram symbolize the union of fire and water, the marriage of soul and spirit, and the alchemical wedding of sulfur and mercury. It is the union of the above and the below, the marriage of heaven and earth, the macrocosm and the microcosm—two things becoming one thing. The harmonious resolution and fusion of opposites represents the completion of the great work and corresponds to the six days of creation—the great work of the absolute.

Ourobouros

THE HEXAGRAM AND THE PLANETS

The mage primarily uses the hexagram in its equation with the seven planets. The attribution of the planets to the hexagram accords with their position on the kabbalistic tree of life (see also pages 36–49 and 80–91). Saturn/Binah takes the position of Daath at the top, being the first sephirah (and the only one of the supernals) to manifest in the macrocosm.

The hexagram is therefore the symbol of the solar system, with the Sun at the center. All planetary energies that the ritual use of the hexagram invokes are therefore different manifestations of constructive, harmonious solar power made available to the mage. The destructive aspects of Mars and Saturn, for example, cannot manifest through the hexagram. In this way, the hexagram also acts as a shield against disruptive astral energies.

Symbolism

The one: The hexagram as a whole symbolizes the one, often emphasized by enclosing it within the ourobouros (the dragon or serpent eating its own tail that represents the eternal cycle of nature).

The duad: The two composite triangles symbolize the unity of fire and water, above and below.

The trinity: Soul, spirit, and body are implicit in the repeated triangles.

The quaternity: The alchemical symbols of the four elements—fire, air, water, and earth—appear in the crossing triangles.

The quintessence: The fifth element of spirit is implicit as the mystic center, the manifesting source of energy and intelligence that is found through meditating on the hexagram as a mandala.

The hexad: The six points denote the six directions— north, south, east, west, above, and below—that, as pairs, define the three dimensions (soul, spirit, and body) within which the great work takes place.

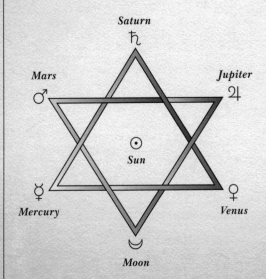

Saturn ♄

Mars ♂

Jupiter ♃

☉ Sun

Mercury ☿

Venus ♀

Moon ☽

The lesser ritual of the hexagram

Perform this ritual as a form of meditation on the symbolism of the hexagram, or before and after the greater ritual of the hexagram (see pages 72–73).

Isis

INRI

This rite centers around the letters INRI, the Latin abbreviation for Jesus of Nazareth, king of the Jews. The Hebrew letters also correspond to the paths of the tree of life. The path related to the letter yod (I) is linked with Virgo, that of nun (N) to Scorpio, and resh (R) to the Sun. Virgo is associated with the Egyptian goddess Isis, Scorpio with Apophis, and the Sun with Osiris. The first letters of these names combine to form IAO, considered by the Gnostics to be the supreme name of God. The signs of Isis, Apophis, and Osiris form the letters LVX—which is Latin for "light."

1. Perform the lesser banishing ritual of the pentagram to make a magic circle (see pages 64–65).

2. Extend your arms like Christ on the cross (the sign of Osiris slain) and say: **"Yod Nun Resh Yod."**

3. Point your right arm straight up with the elbow locked. Bow your head toward your still extended left arm, forming a letter L (the sign of the mourning of Isis), and say: **"Virgo, Isis, mighty mother."** Then throw your head straight back, raise your arms above your head in the shape of a V (the sign of Apophis and Typhon), and say: **"Scorpio, Apophis, destroyer."** Next, cross your right arm over your left arm on your chest, forming a letter X, bow your head (the sign of Osiris risen), and say: **"Sol, Osiris, slain and arisen."**

4. Gradually raise your arms, palms upward, saying: **"Isis, Apophis, Osiris."**

5. With arms fully extended, raise your head as if to the noonday Sun and resonate the divine name of God: **"IAO"** (pronounced Ee-Ah-Oh).

6. Repeat the physical movements described in step 3, saying **"L," "V,"** and **"X"** as each letter is formed. Fold your hands on your chest, bow your head, and say: **"The light of the cross."**

7. Trace the appropriate hexagram in each quarter of the circle (see steps 8–11). Note that the elementary correspondences of the quarters differ from those used with pentagrams, in accordance with the zodiacal order:

North: *Water/Cancer*
South: *Earth/Taurus*
East: *Fire/Aries*
West: *Air/Gemini*

8. Trace the invoking or banishing hexagram of fire in the east. Bring your hand up to your chest, thrust it out as if stabbing the center of the hexagram, and vibrate the word: *"Ararita."* (The letters correspond to the seven planets and stand for "One is his beginning; one his individuality; his permutation is one.")

9. Trace the invoking or banishing hexagram of earth in the south, then thrust toward the center of the hexagram, again vibrating the word: *"Ararita."*

10. Trace the invoking or banishing hexagram of air in the west, then thrust toward the center of the hexagram, again vibrating the word: *"Ararita."*

11. Trace the invoking or banishing hexagram of water in the north, then thrust toward the center of the hexagram, again vibrating the word: *"Ararita."*

12. Repeat steps 2–6, then conclude with the lesser banishing ritual of the pentagram.

Osiris

TRACING THE HEXAGRAMS

Use the wand for tracing invoking hexagrams and the dagger for banishing hexagrams. Alternatively, use the sign of benediction (index and middle finger extended, the other fingers tucked into the palm and covered by the thumb).

Fire-invoking

Fire-banishing

Earth-invoking

Earth-banishing

Air-invoking

Air-banishing

Water-invoking

Water-banishing

The greater ritual of the hexagram

Use this ritual to invoke or banish planets or their related zodiacal signs. You will need to refer to an astrological chart to find out in which quarter the planet is situated at the time of the ritual.

Zodiac symbols and planets

♈ **Aries,** *ruled by Mars*

♉ **Taurus,** *ruled by Venus*

♊ **Gemini,** *ruled by Mercury*

♋ **Cancer,** *ruled by the Moon*

♌ **Leo,** *ruled by the Sun*

♍ **Virgo,** *ruled by Mercury*

♎ **Libra,** *ruled by Venus*

♏ **Scorpio,** *ruled by Mars*

♐ **Sagittarius,** *ruled by Jupiter*

♑ **Capricorn,** *ruled by Saturn*

♒ **Aquarius,** *ruled by Saturn*

♓ **Pisces,** *ruled by Jupiter*

1. *Perform the lesser banishing ritual of the hexagram (see pages 70–71 but omit the concluding lesser banishing ritual of the pentagram).*

2. *Turn to the quarter of the circle in which the planet is situated at the time of the ritual, and trace the relevant invoking or banishing hexagram (see opposite). For example, to invoke Mercury, begin at the lower left corner of the upward-pointing triangle, inscribing the line clockwise to trace the triangle. Then trace the downward-pointing triangle from the top right corner, again working in a clockwise direction. Finish by tracing the astrological symbol of the planet in the center of the hexagram. Banishing hexagrams are performed the other way around and traced counterclockwise.*

3. *If you are invoking or banishing the Sun, you will need to trace all six planetary hexagrams, one on top of another, before drawing the astrological symbol of the Sun in the center. This is because the Sun is not connected with any point of the hexagram.*

4. *If you are invoking or banishing a zodiac sign, use the hexagram of the planet that rules the sign and inscribe the astrological symbol of the sign in the center of the hexagram instead of the planetary symbol.*

5. *While tracing the hexagram and symbol, vibrate the word: "**Ararita.**"*

6. *Perform the lesser banishing ritual of the hexagram (this time omit step 1 only).*

Invoking hexagrams

Banishing hexagrams

Saturn-invoking

Jupiter-invoking

Saturn-banishing

Jupiter-banishing

Venus-invoking

Moon-invoking

Venus-banishing

Moon-banishing

Mercury-invoking

Mars-invoking

Mercury-banishing

Mars-banishing

Planetary symbols

| ♄ | Saturn | ♃ | Jupiter | ♀ | Venus | ☉ | Sun |
| ☽ | Moon | ☿ | Mercury | ♂ | Mars | | |

The secret seven

Geometric representations of the number seven—such as a heptagram (seven-pointed star) or heptagon (seven-sided polygon)—provide fascinating and satisfying examples of the harmony of the planets.

Days of the week

A seven-pointed star provides the sequence of the seven days of the week, starting at the Moon and crossing over to Mars, then Mercury, Jupiter, Venus, Saturn, the Sun, and back to the Moon. The names of the days still preserve their planetary connotations, particularly in the Latin tongues:

- *Sunday—Sun.*
- *Lundi (Monday)—Moon (la lune/luna).*
- *Mardi (Tuesday)—Mars.*
- *Mercredi (Wednesday)— Mercury.*
- *Jueves (Thursday)—Jupiter.*
- *Vendredi (Friday)—Venus.*
- *Saturday—Saturn.*

To explore the relationships between the planets, place the Sun at the top angle of a heptagon or heptagram, followed counterclockwise by Venus, Mercury, the Moon, Saturn, Jupiter, and Mars.

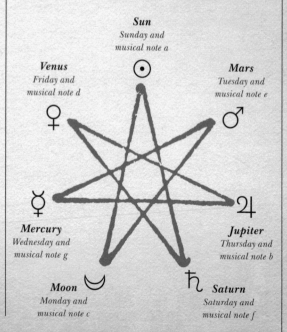

Sun
Sunday and musical note a

Venus
Friday and musical note d

Mars
Tuesday and musical note e

Mercury
Wednesday and musical note g

Jupiter
Thursday and musical note b

Moon
Monday and musical note c

Saturn
Saturday and musical note f

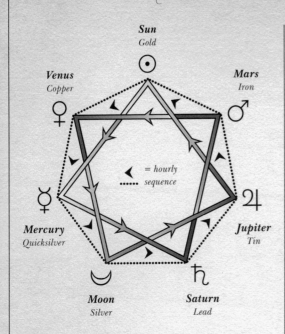

Sun
Gold

Venus
Copper

Mars
Iron

☿ = hourly
······· sequence

Mercury
Quicksilver

Jupiter
Tin

Moon
Silver

Saturn
Lead

CLASSICAL METALS

The seven planets equate to the seven classical metals of antiquity. Here, too, harmonious sequences can be found. Draw a seven-pointed star, starting with Mars/iron, crossing to Venus/copper, then the Moon/silver, Jupiter/tin, the Sun/gold, Mercury/quicksilver, Saturn/lead, and then back to Mars. This sequence describes the increasing atomic numbers of the metals.

❋

Musical sequence

The seven-pointed star also contains a musical sequence. It involves the two consonant musical intervals between two sounds that are one octave apart—namely, the fifth and the third, as counted from the lower octave note. Counting clockwise in a circle, aebfcgda represent a cycle of fifths. Counting along the lines of the star, ac, ce, eg, gb, bd, and df represent a cycle of thirds. Counting clockwise around the points of the star, skipping every alternate point, abcdefga represent the scale.

PLANETARY HOURS

A heptagon provides the sequence of the planetary hours into which each day is divided, working counterclockwise around the heptagon—the hour of the Sun is followed by the hour of Venus, then the hour of Mercury, and so on (see also page 123). To see how this figure connects with other planetary sequences, start at Saturn and work counterclockwise. This describes the Chaldean order of the spheres. This sequence, first observed (supposedly) by the ancient Chaldeans of the Middle East, gives the order of increasing speed of the planets against the fixed stars, as observed from the Earth. This ordering of the planets was superseded, but not invalidated, by the heliocentric theory of the solar system. For the mage as microcosm, the Chaldean order remains entirely valid.

The ogdoadic star

Ogdoadic means "pertaining to the number eight." As the number of Thoth and Mercury, eight is one of the most important numbers in magic.

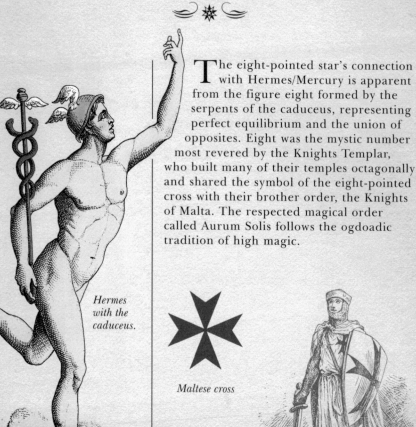

The eight-pointed star's connection with Hermes/Mercury is apparent from the figure eight formed by the serpents of the caduceus, representing perfect equilibrium and the union of opposites. Eight was the mystic number most revered by the Knights Templar, who built many of their temples octagonally and shared the symbol of the eight-pointed cross with their brother order, the Knights of Malta. The respected magical order called Aurum Solis follows the ogdoadic tradition of high magic.

*Hermes
with the
caduceus.*

Maltese cross

*Knight Templar with
a shield bearing the
Maltese cross.*

The rim of the Magician's hat is the lemniscate symbol of eternity—the number 8 on its side.

Symbolism

- *Geometrically, being the product of 2 x 4, eight represents two squares that form an octagon, the intermediary between the square and the circle—symbolizing terrestrial order and eternal order.*
- *Eight is also the number of the initiate who has passed through the seven spheres (from Malkuth to Chesed) on the path of return on the tree of life (see pages 80–91).*
- *Like the musical octave, it represents a completion of the cycle of seven and a new cycle on a higher octave. It therefore symbolizes regeneration, resurrection, palingenesis, and immortality.*

The Star tarot card usually features eight stars, with the largest star having eight main points.

CONNECTIONS WITH THE TAROT

When placed on its side, the number eight is the lemniscate, the symbol of eternity found above the head of the Magician in the tarot. It therefore depicts the eternal cycle of rising and falling, joining and separating. Most tarot decks depict the major arcana card the Star with an eight-pointed star surrounded by seven smaller stars, suggesting the octave of 7 + 1. The card's number is 17, numerologically 1 + 7. At the time when the tarot first appeared, eight corresponded in mystic cosmogony to the fixed stars of the firmament, denoting transcendence of planetary influences. It was also an emblem of the regenerative holy water of baptism, and this is also represented in the card.

Paths of Magical Attainment

As well as the three pillars of high magic, there are many other forms of wisdom and ritual that can be used by the aspiring mage to progress on his or her path of magical attainment. These include kabbalistic exercises based on the tree of life, tarot, angels, and talismans, as well as Buddhist and yoga meditational practices.

Kabbalah, meaning "oral tradition" in Hebrew, evolved from a strain of Jewish mysticism devoted to penetrating the inner meaning of the Torah, the Jewish scriptures. The key symbol of Kabbalah is the tree of life, which provides a model of creation. By meditating on the spheres of the tree, the mage can become more conscious of the true nature of being.

The tree of life

Pathways to God

The Kabbalah explains how the world came into existence from the will of God through a series of emanations from the divine source. The tree of life can be seen as a framework that shows how the supreme, undifferentiated consciousness of the almighty devolves into the self-consciousness of the individual. It also reveals the paths by which we can return to unity with God, by removing those obstacles that limit consciousness.

The tree of life is depicted as an arrangement of ten spheres on three parallel pillars. These spheres are called sephiroth (sephirah in the singular), meaning "splendid lights." The sephiroth can be understood as facets of the divine personality. The highest sphere, Kether, represents divine glory; the lowest sphere, Malkuth, denotes the material world in which the divine light is comparatively dim.

Below Kether on the middle pillar is a nonsphere called Daath, meaning knowledge. This is the abyss, the void, the gulf that separates the manifest from the unmanifest, the finite from the infinite. To reach the sphere of Daath is to attain union with the divine, the true goal of all mystics and mages.

THE SEPHIROTH

1 Kether
2 Chokhmah
3 Binah
4 Chesed
5 Geburah
6 Tiphareth
7 Netzach
8 Hod
9 Yesod
10 Malkuth

The "nonsphere" below Kether (1) is Daath.

The four planes

The sephiroth exist on four planes. All of the sephiroth inhabit two of the planes except Malkuth (sphere 10), which is only present in the world of action. The four planes are:

- Atziluth, the world of emanation.
- Briah, the world of creation.
- Yetzirah, the world of formation.
- Assiah, the world of action.

The love triangle

The three highest spheres, forming a triangle on the tree, are called the supernals. They are highly abstract emanations of divinity and beyond the apprehension of human intellect alone.

KETHER (1)

Kether is the highest sphere, standing alone as the crown on top of the middle pillar of the tree. It is the sphere of God as the creator. It is the divine glory, the light of which the Sun is but a pale reflection. The first creative act of God is to separate the light from the dark. This separation produces the first pair of opposites, Chokhmah and Binah.

1. Kether correspondences

Meaning: Crown

Element: Root of air

Color: Brilliant white

Magical image: Old, bearded king in profile

Achievement: Divine union

Illusion: Attainment

Virtue: Completion of the great work

Vice: None

Tarot cards: The aces

Chakra: Sahasrara (crown of head)

Keywords: Unity, all, pure consciousness, godhead, beginning, source

Divine name: Eheieh (I am)

Archangel: Metatron

Angelic choir: Chioth ha Qadesh

Material manifestations: Primum mobile (prime mover), nebulae

Magical image for Kether.

2. Chokhmah correspondences

Meaning: Wisdom

Element: Root of fire

Color: Gray

Magical image: Bearded patriarch

Achievement: The vision of God face to face

Illusion: Independence

Virtue: Devotion

Vice: None

Tarot cards: The twos

Chakra: Ajna (between the eyes)

Keywords: Pure creative energy, life force, wellspring

Divine name: Yahweh (lord)

Archangel: Ratziel

Angelic choir: Auphanim

Material manifestation: Zodiac

Magical image for Chokhmah.

3. Binah correspondences

Meaning: Understanding

Element: Root of water

Color: Black

Magical image: Queen mother

Achievement: Vision of sorrow

Illusion: Death

Virtue: Silence

Vices: Inertia, avarice

Tarot cards: The threes

Chakra: Ajna (between the eyes)

Keywords: Limitation, karma, time and space, law, death

Divine name: Yahweh Elohim (lord god)

Archangel: Tzaphqiel

Angelic choir: Aralim

Material manifestation: Saturn

CHOKHMAH (2) AND BINAH (3)

These spheres are the original couple, the father and mother of the universe, the root of all polarity—positive and negative, male and female, yin and yang, respectively. Chokhmah and Binah top the active (right) and passive (left) pillars of the tree, respectively.

Chokhmah is the active father of fathers; Binah, the great mother. The dynamic tension between Binah, God's passive understanding, and Chokhmah, God's active wisdom, produces the divine creative spark. This spark, drawn by Chokhmah from the divine source of Kether, is the seed of life that is received by Binah and generates all the forms in the universe.

Magical image for Binah.

The ethical triangle

The second triangle on the tree is a reflection of the supernal triangle (the three highest spheres).

CHESED (4) AND GEBURAH (5)

Below Chokhmah on the right pillar of the tree is Chesed, the sphere of mercy or love. Chesed is the constructive and organizing energy that builds the blueprints for all forms that are latent in Binah. In opposition to Chesed is Geburah, on the left pillar of the tree. Geburah is the sphere of severity or strength and imposes the limitations of mortality on all created things. Whereas Binah is the mother of all forms, Geburah is the destroyer. This may seem cruel, but these limitations are an inevitable part of the deal. They mean that created forms are finite in the manifest world of time and space. This is the principle of change, without which there is stasis.

4. Chesed correspondences

Meaning: Mercy

Element: Water

Color: Blue

Magical image: Magnificent enthroned king

Achievement: Vision of love

Illusion: Self-righteousness

Virtue: Obedience

Vices: Tyranny, hypocrisy, bigotry, gluttony, waste

Tarot cards: The fours

Chakra: Vissudha (throat)

Keywords: Authority, creativity, inspiration, vision, leadership

Divine name: El (him)

Archangel: Tzadkiel

Angelic choir: Chasmalim

Material manifestation: Jupiter

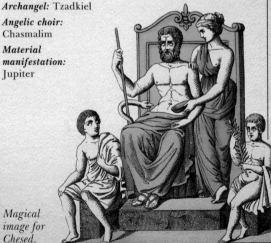

Magical image for Chesed.

5. Geburah correspondences

Meanings: Strength, severity

Element: Fire

Color: Scarlet

Magical image: Mighty warrior in a chariot

Achievement: Vision of power

Illusion: Invincibility

Virtues: Courage, loyalty

Vices: Cruelty, destruction

Tarot cards: The fives

Chakra: Vissudha (throat)

Keywords: Power, courage, domination, passion

Divine name: Elohim Gevor (almighty god)

Archangel: Camael

Angelic choir: Seraphim

Material manifestation: Mars

Magical image for Geburah.

6. Tiphareth correspondences

Meaning: Beauty

Element: Air

Color: Yellow

Magical images: Shining king, divine child, sacrificed god

Achievement: Vision of harmony

Illusion: Identification

Virtues: Devotion to the great work, integrity

Vices: Pride, self-importance

Tarot cards: The sixes

Chakra: Anahata (heart)

Keywords: Harmony, integrity, balance, wholeness, the self, self-sacrifice

Divine name: Yahweh Eloah va Daath (lord god of knowledge)

Archangels: Raphael, Michael

Angelic choir: Malachim

Material manifestation: Sun

TIPHARETH (6)

Balancing Chesed and Geburah is Tiphareth, situated below Kether and Daath on the middle pillar. Meaning beauty, Tiphareth is the reflection of Kether. Whereas Kether represents supreme consciousness, Tiphareth symbolizes consciousness of consciousness—it is the birth of self-consciousness in creation. Tiphareth is the visible glory of God made manifest, representing vitality and the will to live. It is the balancing point, the heart of the tree, the heart of creation, just as the Sun is the heart of the solar system.

Magical image for Tiphareth.

The lower sephiroth

The lower triangle on the tree reflects a further organization of the preceding pattern. At the base is a single sphere, Malkuth.

NETZACH (7) AND HOD (8)

Netzach, at the base of the right pillar, is the positive force of attraction and cohesion in the universe. It is the sphere of animal drives, sensuality, passion, instinctive responses, and the natural as opposed to the contrived. Its opposite sphere, Hod, forms the base of the left pillar and represents the duplicity that results from self-consciousness. It is the sphere of mental faculties, intelligence, reason, and considered responses, the artificial, ambivalent, and contrived. Hod is the negative force behind flux and change.

7. Netzach correspondences

Meaning: Victory

Element: Fire

Color: Emerald

Magical image: Beautiful naked woman

Achievement: Vision of beauty triumphant

Illusion: Projection

Virtue: Unselfishness

Vices: Lust, wantonness

Tarot cards: The sevens

Chakra: Manipuraka (solar plexus)

Keywords: Empathy, sympathy, pleasure, luxury, sensuality, desire, lust

Divine name: Yahweh Tzabaoth (lord of hosts)

Archangel: Haniel

Angelic choir: Elohim

Material manifestation: Venus

Magical image for Netzach.

8. Hod correspondences

Meaning: Glory

Element: Water

Color: Orange

Magical image: Hermaphrodite

Achievement: Vision of splendor

Illusion: Order

Virtue: Truthfulness

Vice: Falsehood

Tarot cards: The eights

Chakra: Manipuraka (solar plexus)

Keywords: Genius, reason, mediation, communication, self-knowledge, ambivalence

Divine name: Elohim Tzabaoth (god of hosts)

Archangels: Michael, Raphael

Angelic choir: Beni Elohim

Material manifestation: Mercury

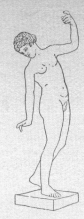

Magical image for Hod.

9. Yesod correspondences

Meaning: Foundation

Element: Air

Color: Violet

Magical image: Beautiful, powerful, naked man

Achievement: Vision of the machinery of the universe

Illusion: Security

Virtue: Independence

Vices: Idleness, sloth

Tarot cards: The nines

Chakra: Svadistthana (genitals)

Keywords: Perception, imagination, emotion

Divine name: Shaddai el Chai (almighty living god)

Archangel: Gabriel

Angelic choir: Cherubim

Material manifestation: Moon

YESOD (9)

Balancing the polarity of flux and cohesion is Yesod, the penultimate sephirah on the middle pillar. Yesod rules the constant, ordered cycles of time, as seen in the regularly changing phases of the Moon. The reproductive cycles of all things on Earth are regulated by the Moon, as are the tides of the oceans. Yesod is both fluid and precise, ruling the unconscious mind and emotions on one hand and organizing the machinery of the universe on the other.

Magical image for Yesod.

MALKUTH (10)

Although the last sephirah, Malkuth, meaning kingdom, appears to be at the bottom of the tree, it is actually the cherry on top, for the roots of the tree are beyond the vanishing point of Kether—this tree grows out of heaven, not earth. The magical image of Malkuth is a young woman crowned and throned. She is both the daughter and the bride of God, but she is exiled in matter, separated from her consort by the gulf of creation. In this sense, God himself is exiled from an aspect of himself. His queen, mother earth, who has borne his children, is known as the Shekinah.

10. Malkuth correspondences

Meaning: Kingdom

Element: Earth

Colors: Citrine, olive, russet, black

Magical image: A young woman crowned and throned

Achievement: Vision of the holy guardian angel

Illusion: Materialism

Virtue: Discrimination

Vices: Avarice, inertia

Tarot cards: The tens

Chakra: Muladhara (feet)

Keywords: Material, solid, nature, heavy

Divine name: Adonai ha Aretz (lord of the earth)

Archangel: Sandalphon

Angelic choir: Ishim

Material manifestations: Elements

Magical image for Malkuth.

THE SHEKINAH

The Shekinah is sometimes called the liberating angel, whom Jacob in Genesis 48:16 refers to as "the angel that redeemed me from all evil." The Shekinah is also the guardian of the tree of life in the garden of Eden. Gershom Scholem, a great scholar of Jewish mysticism, tells us that the Shekinah was separated from God, her lover, following the fall of Adam and Eve. Only on Friday nights, the eve of the Sabbath, are they reunited before being forced to part again. Not until all the original light of creation has returned to its divine source will the cosmic lovers be permanently reunited. Scholem writes: "To lead the Shekinah back to God and to unite her with Him is the true purpose of the Torah." We are all involved in this process. Every act of love and compassion brings the heavenly couple closer together. In this sense, life is a love story. In essence, we are all lonely lovers separated from our love, which can only be found at the very heart of our being.

Every act of love returns the Shekinah closer to God.

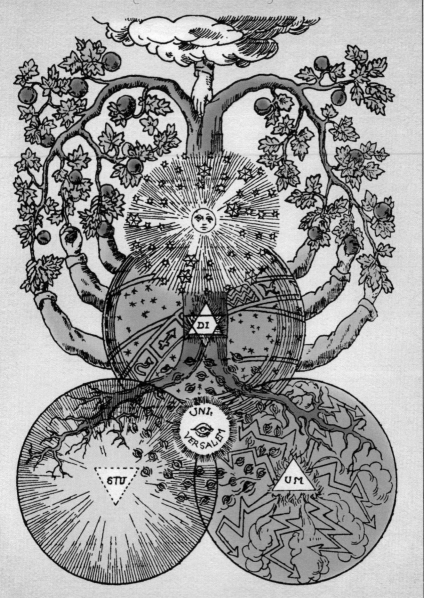

The tree of knowledge of good and evil from *Secret Symbols of the Rosicrucians*, 1785, a compendium of alchemical and mystical wisdom. The Shekinah is the guardian of the tree.

Ritual exercises

Human beings are microcosms of the tree of life. You can incorporate the tree's attributes into your being by regularly performing ritual exercises.

The kabbalistic cross of light

Performing this exercise will help you feel the power of the tree of life resonate through your body. It is often incorporated into more complex rituals, such as consecrating magical implements (see pages 28–31). Use the sign of benediction to draw the cross on your body (index and middle finger extended, with the other fingers tucked into the palm and covered by the thumb).

1. *Stand facing the east, and imagine a brilliant white light above you. Raise your hand above your head and draw the light down to your forehead, saying:*

    *"**Ateh**" (pronounced Ah-tay; meaning unto thee).*

2. *Bring the line of light down to your breast and say:*

    *"**Iao**" (Ee-ah-oh; that I am or my true self).*

3. *Draw the light down through your body, and as you point toward your feet, say:*

    *"**Malkuth**" (Mahl-kooth; the kingdom).*

4. *Bring the line of light up to your right shoulder, saying:*

    *"**Ve Geburah**" (Veh Geb-oo-rah; the power).*

5. *Draw the line across to your left shoulder, saying:*

    *"**Ve Gedulah**" (Veh Ged-oo-lah; the glory).*

6. *Feel the great cross of light running through you, then cup your hands to your heart and say:*

    *"**Le Olahm, Amen**" (Leh Oh-lahm, Ah-men; for all time, Amen).*

The middle pillar exercise

1. *Facing west, visualize the black pillar of severity on your right side and the white pillar of mercy on your left side. Imagine the black pillar is reflected in your left side and the white pillar in your right side.*

2. *Now begin the process of vibrating the divine names at the chakra points, vibrating each name several times if necessary until it fills your whole being. Start by visualizing a flaming sphere of brilliant white light at your Kether point, a few inches above your head. Inhale deeply and vibrate the divine name:*

   "Eheieh" *(pronounced Eh-heh-yeh).*

3. *Bring down the light from above and visualize a flaming sphere of bright yellow at your heart center, the Tiphareth point. Feel the warmth of your interior sun radiating through you. Inhale deeply and vibrate the divine name:*

   "Yahweh Eloah va Daath" *(Yah-way Eh-loh-ah vah Dah-Ath).*

4. *Bring down the light and visualize a flaming sphere of bright violet at your genital region, Yesod. Inhale deeply and vibrate the divine name:*

   "Shaddai el Chai" *(Shah-dye el Hai).*

5. *Bring down the light and visualize a flaming sphere of bright emerald at your feet, Malkuth. Inhale deeply and vibrate the divine name:*

   "Adonai ha Aretz" *(Ah-doh-nye ha Ah-retz).*

6. *Finish by performing the kabbalistic cross of light (see opposite). This helps to balance the energy that you have absorbed.*

O ne of the key ritual exercises in high magic, the middle pillar exercise vibrates the divine names of the middle pillar sephiroth at the chakra points in the body to which they correspond (chakra, meaning "wheel of light" in Sanskrit, is an energy center in the body according to yoga philosophy). By performing this exercise on a regular basis, you will become increasingly attuned to the energies of the sephiroth and start to embody the splendor of the tree of life.

The tarot can be used to divine the underlying dynamics of the mage's relationship with life. Used in structured layouts, known as spreads, the cards can trigger intuitive and inspired responses to situations that you wish to understand more fully. The sheer depth and richness of their symbolism make them an inexhaustible source of inspiration and intuition.

The tarot

The Devil major arcana card from the medieval Marseilles tarot deck.

The origins of tarot cards remain steeped in mystery. Packs of cards for gambling and fortune-telling were first referred to around 1370. The standard tarot deck as we know it today, with 22 trump cards (major arcana) and 56 suit cards (minor arcana), dates back to around 1500 and first appeared in northern Italy.

Although the tarot has become one of the principal keys of high magic, it was not until the late eighteenth century that there was evidence that the tarot was included in the hermetic arts. In 1773, Frenchman Antoine Court de Gébelin speculated that they were of ancient Egyptian origin, and a contemporary of his called Alliette named them the Book of Thoth. However, it was the great French mage Eliphas Lévi who accorded them their preeminent significance with the publication of his deeply influential work *The Dogma and Ritual of High Magic* in 1856.

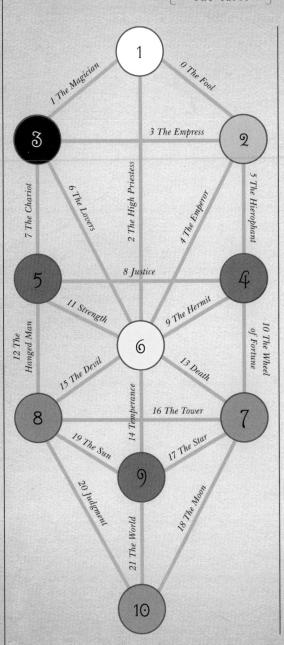

Tarot and the Kabbalah

Whatever their origins, the tarot appears custom-made for kabbalistic magic. The number of major arcana cards (22) equals the number of letters in the Hebrew alphabet and the number of paths on the tree of life. The ten sephiroth correspond with the minor arcana, sphere 1 relating to the four aces and so on.

	Sephiroth	**Tarot**
1	Kether	Aces
2	Chokhmah	Twos
3	Binah	Threes
4	Chesed	Fours
5	Geburah	Fives
6	Tiphareth	Sixes
7	Netzach	Sevens
8	Hod	Eights
9	Yesod	Nines
10	Malkuth	Tens

The major arcana

There are 22 major arcana cards, numbered 0–21. Each card has a
title and bears a symbolic image. Cards with traditional imagery based
on the medieval Marseilles tarot deck are pictured here; different decks
can vary, but the meanings remain the same. Cards 8 and 11, Justice
and Strength, are sometimes transposed. The major arcana can be
used as a focus for meditation. See page 103 to learn how
to use them for divination.

0. The Fool

A colorfully garbed young man appears lost in
a daydream. His face is turned to the sky, and he
carries a staff over his shoulder with a small bundle
of possessions. He is ready to set forth in search of
life's secrets. He is oblivious to danger, because he
knows that he cannot go wrong. Everything is right—
life is eternal, and he is immortal. If he embarks on
the journey, his last step as a child of innocence will
be his first as a man of experience.

1. The Magician

A dignified young man stands before a table arrayed
with the four magical implements. In one hand, he
holds aloft a wand; with the other hand, he points
to the ground, indicating his intent to integrate the
powers of above with those of below. Over his head
is a horizontal figure eight, symbolizing the eternal
joining and separating of perfectly balanced and
unified opposites. The Magician is the balancing
point, mediating between the eternal polarities.

2. The High Priestess

A seated young woman is wearing a horned headdress,
representing the crescent moon. On her lap is an open
book, a symbol of esoteric wisdom and law. Like the
Magician, the High Priestess is a balancing point
between opposing forces, but where he is active,
she is passive.

3. The Empress

An attractive woman is comfortably enthroned,
and behind her head is a circle of stars. At her
side is a shield bearing the symbol of a golden
eagle, representing courage and power.
Surrounded by flowers, the scene suggests
abundance and fertility. Her number is 3,
which stands for the creative union of
opposites—male and female come together
to produce a child.

4. The Emperor

The Emperor is a stern, armored figure,
half-seated on a throne. He represents solidity and
constructive energy. The Emperor holds a scepter in
one hand, a symbol of dominion. His shield is embossed
with a golden eagle, another symbol of dominance.
Without his Empress, the potency of the Emperor
is unfulfilled, his empire devoid of life.

5. The Hierophant

A richly bedecked pontiff raises his right hand
in benediction, while in his left hand he holds a
papal cross. Before him kneel two priests, ready to
receive his blessing. Also known as the High Priest
or the Pope in older packs, this card symbolizes the
authority of established religion.

6. The Lovers

A young man stands between two women, with Cupid poised above with his bow and arrow. The man must make a choice: between the two women, between idealistic love and physical attraction, between vice and virtue. This card symbolizes the themes of trial and choice.

7. The Chariot

A warrior prince with a scepter in his right hand stands in a chariot attached to two horses, which represent emotion that needs to be controlled. The Chariot is a symbol of movement, power, and triumph. The charioteer is a symbol of power and self-mastery.

8. Justice

A majestic female figure holds a sword in her right hand and a pair of scales in her left hand. The double-edged sword represents one edge to condemn and the other to save. The scales symbolize the weighing of good and evil. This card signifies the law of karma, cause and effect: "As a man sows, so shall he reap."

9. The Hermit

A cloaked and bearded elderly man stands motionless. In his right hand is a lantern; in his left hand, a staff. The Hermit is a symbol of withdrawal, concentration, abstention, and self-control. The number 9 symbolizes initiation and completeness. The Hermit is self-contained, his soul illuminated by an inner sun, represented by his lantern.

10. The Wheel of Fortune

The figure on the left crawls down the wheel, representing declining fortunes. The creature on the right creeps upward, symbolizing fortunes rising. The sphinx at the top is armed with a sword, suggesting escape from the wheel of fate. The wheel itself is a symbol of destiny and the eternal processes that underlie human existence.

11. Strength

A young woman gently but firmly opens or closes the mouth of a lion. The fiery, sexual strength and passion of the masculine lion is restrained to the satisfaction of the cool, controlled feminine nature. The card symbolizes potent but contained sexuality and the fortitude required for successful union.

12. The Hanged Man

A young man hangs upside down from one foot. His free leg is bent at the knee to form a symbolic cross. The gallows from which he hangs are formed from two saplings, each with six amputated branches, suggesting the possibility of renewed growth to come. Far from looking tortured, he wears a beatific expression. The essential meaning of the card is illumination through self-sacrifice.

13. Death

The skeletal figure of Death uses a scythe to gather his grisly harvest. However, the field in which he stands is fertile. The mystic white rose symbolizes regeneration, new growth, and the emergence of life from death. Death is not absolute. It marks transformation, major change, and the opportunity for life renewed.

14. Temperence

An angel pours a fluid from one cup into another. This can be seen as the essence of life being poured into a new vessel; alternately, male and female, body and spirit, are comingling. Temperence is the virtue of self-restraint, tempering the desire of the will with the selflessness of humility to achieve equilibrium.

15. The Devil

A grim-faced, bat-winged, half-human figure with the horns and legs of a goat perches on a plinth. The plinth symbolizes worldly domination; the goat represents creative energy but also greed and excess. This card signifies negative power, self-indulgence, and carnal excess.

16. The Tower

The tower is struck by lightning and shows two human figures falling headlong to the ground, symbolizing the fall of the mighty. The ivory tower of conceit is destroyed in a moment of supreme illumination. All false ideas and aspects of personality fall like scales from the eyes of the man who sees clearly for the first time.

17. The Star

A naked maiden kneels by a pool and pours the waters of life from a pitcher in each hand. A large eight-pointed star and seven smaller ones fill the sky. The large star represents regeneration and a new life won through magical attainment. The woman is eternally young, eternally renewing creation, giving life to both mind and matter. In turn, she herself is a manifestation of the ultimate, limitless source of cosmic energy represented by the star.

18. The Moon

Two dogs are howling at the Moon, symbolizing the imagination. Beyond them, a path winds between two towers to a hilly horizon. In the foreground is a pool from which a crayfish emerges onto land. Man's half-evolved nature is drawn toward the reflected light of the imagination. Behind is the depth of the unconscious, from which nameless things emerge.

19. The Sun

Two youths stand in a walled garden beneath a many-rayed sun, shining down on them and dropping the dew of its bounty on the ground. The card represents the full light of understanding that completes the evolutionary cycle—the restoration of innocence but with the balance of wisdom.

20. Judgment

An angel blows his trumpet from the heavens, surrounded by a circle of cloud symbolizing the cycle of birth and death. A man, woman, and child emerge from the water, hands clasped in prayer. Their nakedness indicates that they have nothing to conceal, suggesting a life well spent. Although summoned to judgment, they can look forward to rebirth in a new life.

21. The World

A dancer is framed by a laurel wreath, which suggests victory, the universe, totality, and wholeness. Around the wreath are a lion, a bull, an angel, and an eagle, representing north, south, east, and west. The dancer has a wistful countenance, for she feels the sufferings of the world, but her dance is one of joyous celebration. She signifies success, triumphant conclusion, completion, and reward.

The minor arcana

The minor arcana are used with the major arcana for divination (see page 103). There are 56 cards divided into four suits: swords, wands, cups, and pentacles. Each suit comprises four court cards—king, queen, knight, and page—and ten pip cards numbered ace to ten.

THE COURT CARDS

The court cards usually apply to real people involved in the situation being explored. The page is a boy or girl under age 21, the knight is a man aged 21–34, the queen is a woman over age 21, and the king is a man over age 35.

Significator card

When using the tarot for divination, a significator card is sometimes selected to represent (signify) the person having the reading (the querent). The significator is usually chosen from the court cards according to the querent's age, coloring, and/or personality.

Page of swords

Knight of wands

Queen of cups

King of pentacles

Swords

The suit of swords corresponds to the element air. Being a weapon, the sword suggests conflict, cruelty, pain, and suffering. The suit therefore tends to indicate misfortune, and two or more appearing in a spread is ominous.

Two and five of swords.

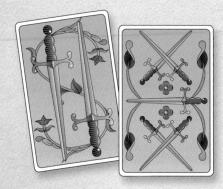

Wands

The suit of wands (also known as batons, rods, staffs, or scepters) is related to the element fire. It signifies the masculine principle, the will, and creative energy. When wands appear in a spread, they tend to relate to enterprise, initiative, and progress.

Three and eight of wands.

Sword meanings

Ace: Root of the powers of air

Two: Peace

Three: Sorrow

Four: Truce

Five: Defeat

Six: Science

Seven: Futility

Eight: Interference

Nine: Cruelty

Ten: Ruin

Court cards: People with dark brown or black hair; dark skin; dark brown or black eyes; and/or a bright personality

Wand meanings

Ace: Root of the powers of fire

Two: Dominion

Three: Virtue

Four: Completion

Five: Strife

Six: Victory

Seven: Valor

Eight: Swiftness

Nine: Strength

Ten: Oppression

Court cards: People with light or dark brown hair; light olive skin; brown, green, or hazel eyes; and/or a fiery personality

Cup meanings

Ace: Root of the powers of water

Two: Love

Three: Abundance

Four: Luxury

Five: Disappointment

Six: Pleasure

Seven: Debauch

Eight: Indolence

Nine: Happiness

Ten: Satiety

Court cards: People with blond, light brown, or gray hair; fair to medium skin; blue or gray eyes; and/or a sensitive personality

Pentacle meanings

Ace: Root of the powers of earth

Two: Change

Three: Work

Four: Power

Five: Worry

Six: Success

Seven: Failure

Eight: Prudence

Nine: Gain

Ten: Wealth

Court cards: People with red, light blond, or gray hair; fair or freckled skin; blue or gray eyes; and/or an earthy personality

Cups

The suit of cups (also known as chalices) is the luckiest suit. It corresponds to the element water. Cups symbolize the feminine principle, love, marriage, emotions, sensitivity, and pleasure when they appear in a spread.

Four and nine of cups.

Pentacles

The suit of pentacles (also called disks or coins) corresponds to the element earth. It relates to all material concerns, including money, property, status, and security.

Ace and seven of pentacles.

Using the tarot for divination

Divination means "seeking to understand the hidden," and can be used to explore everyday situations. The person giving the reading is known as the reader; the person having the reading is referred to as the querent.

The celtic cross

The celtic cross tarot spread provides a good balance of the dynamics that come to play in almost any situation. The reader starts by choosing a significator card (0), removing it from the deck and placing it in the center of the table. The querent then shuffles the deck and cuts it into three piles. After that, the reader restacks them in reverse order and deals out the top ten cards into the appropriate positions.

0 The significator: Represents the querent.

1 The cover: Important influences around the current situation.

2 The cross: Obstacles that the querent must deal with.

3 The root: The root cause of the situation.

4 The past: Influences from the recent past.

5 The crown: The best that can be achieved from current circumstances.

6 The future: Fresh influences about to come into play.

7 The querent: The way the querent relates to the situation.

8 The house: The way people around the querent affect matters.

9 Hopes and fears: The querent's hopes, fears, and expectations.

10 The outcome: The answer to the question.

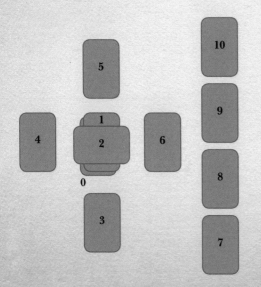

The mage engages with many spirits, the most important of
which are the angels of the heavenly host. This section considers
the angelic choirs and ruling angels associated with the spheres
of the tree of life. The mage who can summon angels
for help is blessed with great power.

Angelic magic

Angelology is a complex subject that
has been studied for millennia. The
tradition is shared by Judeo-Christian,
Islamic, and hermetic traditions, developed
from the much older traditions of the
ancient Egyptians, Chaldeans, Babylonians,
and Zoroastrians. All of them agree that
different groups, or choirs, of angels are
arranged hierarchically in much the same
manner as the sephiroth on the tree of life
of the Kabbalah (see pages 80–89). Only
the angels of the kabbalistic traditions
are discussed in detail here.

Kabbalistic angelic hierarchy

	Tree of life sephiroth	Kabbalistic angelic choirs
1	Kether	Chioth ha Qadesh
2	Chokhmah	Auphanim
3	Binah	Aralim
4	Chesed	Chasmalim
5	Geburah	Seraphim
6	Tiphareth	Malachim
7	Netzach	Elohim
8	Hod	Beni Elohim
9	Yesod	Cherubim
10	Malkuth	Ishim

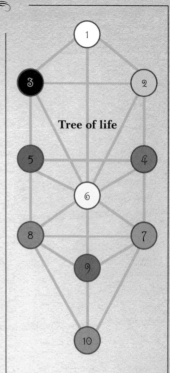

Tree of life

Christian angelic hierarchy

The best-known Christian angelic hierarchy was devised in the late fifth or early sixth century by Pseudo-Dionysius the Areopagite, a Syrian monk, who elaborated this system in his work De Coelesti Hierarchia (The Celestial Hierarchies). *It became established in Western culture as the classic work on the subject, and was adopted in the epic angel sagas of Dante and Milton. The system consists of nine choirs of angels grouped into three triads:*

- **First triad:** *Seraphim, Cherubim, and Thrones.*
- **Second triad:** *Dominions, Virtues, and Powers.*
- **Third triad:** *Principalities, Archangels, and Angels.*

	Christian angelic choirs
1	Seraphim
2	Cherubim
3	Thrones
4	Dominions
5	Virtues
6	Powers
7	Principalities
8	Archangels
9	Angels

THE KABBALISTIC
ANGELIC HIERARCHY

1. Chioth ha Qadesh

The supreme order of angels that gaze upon the
sphere of Kether, the greater countenance of God,
is known as Chioth ha Qadesh. Its angels are also
known as the holy living creatures. Their archangel
is Metatron, referred to as "He who bringeth others
before the face of God." Metatron is the youngest of all
angels, and tradition has it that he was once the biblical
patriarch Enoch. The Talmud says that Metatron is the
link between God and humanity. He may therefore be
invoked, despite the fact that Kether itself is beyond
the mage's reach.

*As God's mediator with men,
the archangel Metatron of the
Chioth ha Qadesh is sometimes
credited as being the angel
who stopped Abraham from
sacrificing his son Isaac
in Genesis 22.*

2. Auphanim

The Auphanim are known as the whirling forces.
These are the angels of Chokhmah, ruled by the
archangel Ratziel, the prince of knowledge of hidden
things, also called the angel of mysteries. The legendary
Book of the Angel Ratziel was said to contain a secret code
that held the keys to the mystery of the world, which
not even any other angel knew.

*According to one tradition, the
book of the archangel Ratziel
of the Auphanim was given
to Noah, who used its secret
knowledge to build the ark in
preparation for the great flood.*

3. Aralim

The Aralim are the strong and mighty ones. These 70,000 angels are made of white fire and serve the sephirah of Binah, the sphere of the eternal female principle. Their leader is the archangel Tzaphqiel, the prince of spiritual strife against evil, whose name means "contemplation of God." When invoking Tzaphqiel, it is appropriate to say, "I allow Binah to show me her true nature." Binah's symbol is the vesica piscis, the pointed oval formed by two overlapping circles.

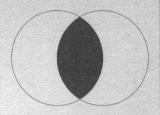

The pointed oval shape formed by a pair of overlapping circles is the vesica piscis symbol, which is related to the Aralim.

4. Chasmalim

The brilliant ones serve Jupiter in the sphere of justice, corresponding to Chesed on the tree of life. The ruler of the Chasmalim is the archangel Tzadkiel, prince of mercy and beneficence, who is also a guard of the gates of the east wind. He may therefore be invoked from that quarter when the position of Jupiter is not known. When invoking Tzadkiel through Chesed, the sephirah may be addressed as follows: "O thou great one, whose name is mighty and whose nature is just, rule in me that I may show forth thy mercy." Chesed's symbol is the pyramid or royal orb.

The symbol of a royal orb is related to the Chasmalim.

5. Seraphim

The Seraphim are the flaming ones, the avenging angels of destruction who serve the sephirah of Geburah, the sphere of the fear of God. Their archangel, Camael (whose name means "he who sees God"), bears the flaming sword, the symbol of Geburah. As the prince of strength and courage, he may impart these qualities if successfully invoked or petitioned. When Geburah is invoked, the mage may say, "O thou most holy, may we pass through thy purging and be clean."

The symbol of a flaming sword is related to the Seraphim.

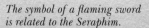

A fifteenth-century gold coin depicting the archangel Michael slaying a dragon. Michael is connected to both the Malachim and Beni Elohim.

6. Malachim

Occasionally referred to as the Shinanin, the Malachim are the kings of Tiphareth, the sphere of the solar light, whose symbol is a cube. The Malachim are responsible for the motions and cycles of all the stars and the planets of the universe. They govern all natural laws and are therefore responsible for all miracles that break these laws. They reflect the ideals of virtue, inspiring valor in heroes and grace in saints. Their archangel is traditionally given as Raphael, the angel of healing, with Michael as his lieutenant (these roles are reversed in the sephirah of Hod). Although this does not tally with the planetary or elemental correspondences, Tiphareth is so benignly disposed toward the mage that it can be invoked without reference to the angels. The best solution perhaps is to invoke both angels when invoking either Tiphareth or Hod.

7. Elohim

The Elohim, which means "gods," are ruled by the archangel Haniel, prince of love and harmony, which are two qualities of Netzach, the sephirah he serves. The symbol of Netzach is the rose, a plant ruled by the corresponding planet Venus, known in the Kabbalah as nogah, meaning "external splendor."

8. Beni Elohim

Beni Elohim, the sons of gods, serve the sphere of Hod, whose symbol is a square apron. Michael, whose name means "who is as God," and Raphael are their leading angels. Hod corresponds to the planet Mercury, mediator of art and knowledge.

The symbol of a rose is related to the Elohim.

The Beni Elohim are related to the sphere of art and knowledge.

A belief in guardian angels can be found in many ancient cultures, such as the winged fravashi of the Zoroastrians. Cherubim are the guardian angels of the kabbalistic tradition.

9. Cherubim

The Cherubim, meaning "those who intercede," are the guardian angels of humankind. They are associated with Yesod, the sephirah that rules the sphere of action and of the Moon. Their presiding archangel is Gabriel, whose name means "God is my strength." Gabriel is one of the most revered of all the angels. It was he who appeared to the Virgin Mary and who dictated the Koran to Mohammed. The symbol of Yesod is a pair of footprints.

The symbol of two footprints is related to the Cherubim.

10. Ishim

The lowest order of angels is the Ishim, associated with the sphere of Malkuth, the kingdom, which equates with the Earth on the mundane level. The Ishim are also called the blessed souls and the souls of the just made perfect. In this respect they equate with the bodhisattvas of Buddhism, being saints who choose to assist their fellow humans. The archangel of the Ishim is Sandalphon, whose name means "co-brother." He is the twin of Metatron, the archangel of the Chioth ha Qadesh, and like his brother he was also once a prophet, Elias. The Shekinah (see page 88) is the goddess of Malkuth and shares the same essence as the Virgin Mary, being daughter, bride, and mother of God.

The Ishim can be equated to the bodhisattvas of Buddhism.

Invoking and petitioning angels

Once you are familiar with the relationship between the elements
(see pages 22–23), the planets (see pages 36–49), and the sephiroth
(see pages 81–88), you will be able to invoke the assistance of the angels
to influence matters associated with their spheres of activity. This can
be done using an angelic script such as the Theban alphabet below.

ANGELIC SCRIPT

Over the centuries,
practitioners of high magic
have used various alphabets
that the angels are said to use.
Angels do not write, of course,
but the characters of angelic
scripts hold a specific energy
like any symbol. Angelic script
can be used for writing letters
of petition and inscribing
names or messages on wax
tablets and talismans. One
angelic script that mages
use is the Theban alphabet.
Simply substitute the angelic
characters for our own.

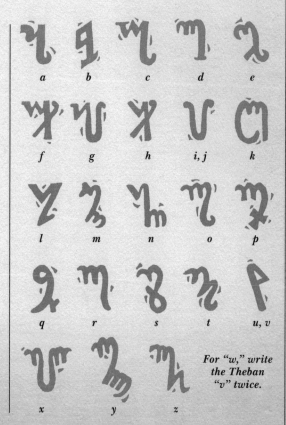

a *b* *c* *d* *e*

f *g* *h* *i, j* *k*

l *m* *n* *o* *p*

q *r* *s* *t* *u, v*

x *y* *z*

*For "w," write
the Theban
"v" twice.*

Petitioning assistance in love

1. Start by performing the lesser banishing ritual of the hexagram (see pages 70–71).

2. Next, invoke the sphere of Venus by inscribing the hexagram of Venus during the greater invoking ritual of the hexagram (see pages 72–73).

3. You may then address the angel directly and term your petition in an appropriate manner, such as by writing your petition using characters from an angelic script (see opposite).

This example demonstrates how to invoke and petition the angels if you wish assistance or clarification in matters of love. In this instance, you may address yourself to the Elohim, invoking the archangel Haniel or one of his assisting angels, such as Kedemel, Hagiel, or Anael, in the sphere of Venus/Netzach. Adapt the ritual according to the subject of your petition.

Evoking angels

An evocation differs from an invocation or a petition in that it represents a request for a specific spirit to appear before the mage. However, this can be difficult to achieve, and great care must be taken with every aspect of the ritual because any mistake can result in an unpleasant, possibly dangerous, experience.

PREPARING FOR AN EVOCATION

When you are ready to attempt an evocation, you should familiarize yourself with the ritual so well that you can visualize everything with your eyes shut. Make a checklist of all necessary items, many of which you may have to make, and have them ready. Immediately before the ritual, purify yourself by bathing.

From the point of view that sees angels as powerful manifestations of psychic energy, an evocation may be said to be a potentially mind-blowing experience, unleashing powerful energies from the unconscious. From the traditional perspective, the mage is drawing into a confined space a spiritual being of enormous energy, the vibrations of which could literally make the walls shake. For these reasons, it is important that you never attempt an evocation until you are fully conversant with invocations, have made successful contact with your personal guardian angel, and have familiarized yourself with the energetic qualities of the angel to be evoked through invocation and prayer.

Connect with the angel through prayer before attempting an evocation.

Evocation of Hagiel

1. *After bathing, put on a green robe and a copper necklace with a green stone, such as jade, malachite, or emerald. Anoint your wrists, breast, and temples with apricot oil mixed with a drop each of sandalwood and cinnamon oils.*

2. *Put a green light bulb in the overhead light of the temple, and sprinkle holy water (see page 57) around the edges of the room.*

3. *In the east quarter of the temple, place a triangle of green silk with equal sides about 18 in. (45 cm) long. On the cloth, place a seven-pointed star cut from green cardboard and inscribed with the sigil for Hagiel (see below and pages 120–127).*

This ritual evokes one of the most beautiful angelic presences, the angel Hagiel, who is connected with Venus, the planet of love and harmony. The ritual bestows the gift of unconditional, unpersonalized love on another person. It is adapted from the work of the great Czech mage Franz Bardon. The ritual should be performed during the hour after sunrise on a Friday, the day and hour of Venus.

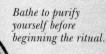

Bathe to purify yourself before beginning the ritual.

Seven-pointed star talisman with the sigil for Hagiel.

Hagiel's color is green, so use green candles to light the temple during the evocation.

4. *Make a circle around the cloth (clockwise) with 49 green stones—49 being Hagiel's number, or 7 (the number of Venus) squared.*

5. *Place a green candle in all four quarters of the temple. Light them and extinguish all other lights except the green light bulb.*

6. *Burn some cinnamon and sandalwood, ideally in a small censer that you can take around the room to suffuse it with Venus-scented smoke.*

7. *Now face the east, with the cloth a few feet in front of you, and perform the lesser banishing ritual of the hexagram (see pages 70–71).*

8. *Facing the quarter where Venus finds itself at the time (which will be the west or north, because Venus is never more than 47° from the Sun), perform the greater invoking ritual of the hexagram of Venus (see pages 72–73).*

9. *Evoke the angel Hagiel by intoning her name silently seven times in your mind: **"Hagiel"** (pronounced Ha-gee-el); then whisper her name seven times; then call her seven times in ringing tones, concluding, equally loudly: **"Come thou before me!"***

Sandalwood

Cinnamon

Evoke Hagiel to bestow the gift of love on another.

10. *If you have been in calm, confident command of the whole process up until this point, you should observe a beautiful feminine form materialize before your eyes. Hagiel does not look the same to everybody, but if she has green eyes you can be sure it is her.*

11. *You will likely be stunned by her presence, but her manner is always sweet and affectionate. Keep control of yourself and ask her to bestow the gift of unconditional love on the person of your choice. If she consents, and she invariably does, you can be sure she will fulfill your wish.*

FINISHING THE RITUAL

Thank Hagiel, and bid her hail and farewell. She will slowly fade from sight. You will not forget her in a hurry and will feel profoundly joyful every time you think of her.

By following the rituals described in this book, you will embark on a process of self-initiation into the true nature of being. One of the most significant experiences on this path is known as the "attainment of the knowledge and conversation of the holy guardian angel." This is a transformational encounter with your inner master, higher self, or guardian angel—the inner divinity within all things.

Self-initiation

An encounter with the inner voice of truth cannot occur without achieving a state of true humility. Christ's words "the meek shall inherit the earth" reveal that higher truth and the knowledge of immortality are only vouchsafed to those who accept their situation in life in the full knowledge of the part they have played in it, aware that they are limited only by their own shortcomings. Such meekness requires what is known as magical equilibrium—perfect balance coupled with great poise. Of course, this is not easily achieved, but there is one exercise, based on yoga philosophy, that can act as a key. The caduceus—the wand of Hermes (see page 13)—perhaps finds its truest expression in Indian yoga.

YOGA

Yoga originated as a Hindu system of philosophy devoted to the union of the self with the supreme being. Hermeticism is sometimes described as Western yoga, since it shares this aim. Yoga employs both physical and mental exercises to achieve states of transcendental consciousness. The quintessence, or secret fire as alchemists also call it, is known in yoga philosophy as prana. It is a subtle energy flowing from the Sun; it contains all the elemental forces and sustains all life on Earth. Prana can be absorbed directly as solar prana, or as reflected energy in the form of lunar prana.

ENERGY CHANNELS

Yoga identifies energy channels within the body, known as nadis. Two of these nadis spiral around a central channel within the spinal cord. The light nadi is called Pingala, the Sun channel. It is masculine, solar, and warming. The dark nadi is called Ida, the Moon channel. It is feminine, lunar, and cooling. The central column is called Sushumna. At its core is the Brahma nadi, the channel for supreme consciousness within the individual.

CHAKRAS

The seven points at which the nadis cross are known as chakras. By bringing Pingala and Ida into conscious balance, the yogi seeks to awaken the serpent power known as Kundalini—the coiled energy that sleeps at the base of the spine—so that it will rise up the Brahma nadi and open the chakras. When the highest chakra is reached, the yogi experiences the supreme consciousness of Brahman, the indestructible and absolute consciousness of the universe.

Links with the caduceus

The parallels between the nadis (energy channels) and the caduceus are immediately apparent. The Pingala and Ida nadis correspond to the masculine and feminine principles, respectively, within all of us, regardless of gender. The Brahma nadi equates to the middle pillar of the kabbalistic tree of life. It is the link between the macrocosm and the microcosm, the channel of individual consciousness.

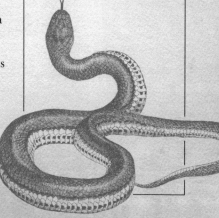

Magical equilibrium

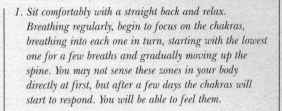

The wand that Hermes holds in his hands is a means for achieving magical equilibrium and attaining union with the absolute, although this is not easily accomplished. It takes sustained attention, practice, commitment, and faith. The way to begin is to connect consciously with the Pingala and Ida energy channels within ourselves. You can do this through a combination of breathing exercise and visualization.

Union with the absolute

This magical exercise is a very powerful one. By identifying the principal energy centers and channels within the body and resonating them with your awareness, you release great amounts of latent energy.

1. Sit comfortably with a straight back and relax. Breathing regularly, begin to focus on the chakras, breathing into each one in turn, starting with the lowest one for a few breaths and gradually moving up the spine. You may not sense these zones in your body directly at first, but after a few days the chakras will start to respond. You will be able to feel them.

2. Next, focus your attention on inhaling the "Sun breath" through your right nostril (close the other nostril with a finger if this helps). Inhale from the bottom of your lungs, imagining that your breath is following the course of the Pingala channel.

3. Switch your attention to the left nostril and allow your breath to follow the course of the Ida nadi, which channels the "Moon breath." Practice for a few minutes twice a day. Soon, you will be able to breathe from the bottom of the channels and feel the energy following your breath and weaving through the chakras.

4. Once you have been successful with the Sun and Moon breaths, focus on both snaking channels at the same time. When you can imagine the two channels of energy rising simultaneously and feel them flowing through your energized chakras, you are well on the way to achieving inner balance.

5. When both the Ida and Pingala nadis are perfectly balanced, resonate the Sushumna nadi and sense the Kundalini serpent begin to uncoil from the base of the spine and vibrate the chakras of the middle pillar. When you can feel the caduceus flowing within your very being, you will find yourself increasingly at peace with yourself and at one with the world. The slumbering serpent will start to awaken within you and reveal itself as the secret fire, which is none other than the logos, the word of God, which will speak to you when you are still enough to receive it.

Divine inspiration

The energy released by this exercise must be allowed to flow freely like a river, or pressure will build up with potentially turbulent results. Any blockages within you, such as repressed memories or anxieties, must be identified and removed. This process can be upsetting, so be gentle with yourself. Have faith— everything that comes up must be released and is better out than in, but you must surrender to the process. Each breath that you take in is an inspiration, full of divine energy. Each breath that you release is an expiration, a surrendering of used energy.

THE SEVEN CHAKRAS

 Sahasrara
(crown of head)

 Ajna
(between the eyes)

 Vissudha
(throat)

 Anahata
(heart)

 Manipuraka
(solar plexus)

 Svadhistthana
(genitals)

 Muladhara
(feet)

One of the most powerful tools of the mage is the talisman. A talisman represents a specific requirement, a wish that the mage wants to have fulfilled. It is a specially designed object that has been magically prepared and charged with power. There are many different ways to do this; the use of Hebrew numerology is described here.

Talismans

Detail from Albrecht Durer's 1514 engraving Melencolia I, which features a 4 x 4 magic square above the angel.

Numerology is the art of using numbers as a key to understanding the relationship between all things and fundamental principles. The numerology method traditionally applied to the making of talismans in high magic uses the kabbalistic technique of gematria. Each Hebrew letter represents a number and vice versa. Gematria consists of adding up the number values of the letters in a word. Words that add up to the same number have a connection. To give a neat example, the Hebrew word for "corpse" has the same numerical value as the word for "to extinguish." Other connections may be less easy to fathom and only perceived through deep contemplation. Such efforts are never futile, no matter how tenuous a perceived connection may appear, because one of the principal aims of the mage is to understand the relationships among all things.

Sh	L	G	R	K	B	Q	Y	A
300	30	3	200	20	2	100	10	1
M*	S	V	K*	N	H	Th	M	D
600	60	6	500	50	5	400	40	4
Tz*	Tz	T	P*	P	Ch	N*	O	Z
900	90	9	800	80	8	700	70	7

* when final letter of a word

THE AIQ BEKAR

Systems of kabbalistic gematria come
in several different types, most of them
grouped under the heading temurah, which
means "permutation." The one commonly
used to make magical talismans is a number/
letter arrangement known as Aiq Bekar
(see above), or the Kabbalah of the nine
chambers, which divides the alphabet
into nine groups according to letter value.
The system derives its name from the first
six letters of the top row (Hebrew is written
from right to left and has few vowels).
In talismanic magic, Aiq Bekar is used
to allocate a numerical value to the letters
in the Hebrew name of a spirit or angel.

MAGIC SQUARES

To turn the series of numbers produced
by the Aiq Bekar into the sigil (symbol) of
a spirit or angel, you need to use a magic
square, known in Kabbalah as a kamea.
Magic squares have been used for thousands
of years in India and China, where they
probably originated. Their first appearance
in the West was in the work of the great
alchemist of Baghdad, Jabir (circa 721–815),
but it was probably kabbalists who first
applied their use to talismanic angel magic.

*Kamea for the Sun and
its planetary seal.*

Kameas

*Kameas (magic squares) are a
series of numbers in a square
grid, cunningly arranged so
that each row, column, and
(usually) diagonal adds up to
the same number. Each planet
has a kamea of increasing
complexity, according to its
position on the tree of life.
A planetary seal is a sigil
that touches all of the numbers
on the kamea.*

Planetary talismans

Magic squares can be used to make a talisman to attract the qualities and energies associated with a particular planet.

Spirits and intelligences

Each planet has an associated spirit and intelligence whose specific influences you can call upon using the planetary talisman. For example, the spirit of the Sun is Sorath; its intelligence is Nakhiel. The planetary intelligences are more personal, guiding, and inspirational, whereas the planetary spirits tend to represent the energy or force itself. So, if you wish to increase your physical vitality, then Sorath, the spirit of the Sun, would be the most useful. If you wish to improve your creativity, then Nakhiel, the intelligence of the Sun, would be preferable.

The Sun governs growth and creativity, so a Sun talisman would be suitable if you require help in any activity related to these aspects.

First, you need to decide which planet you wish to connect with. For example, the Sun's influence on the human sphere corresponds to notions such as vitality, rulership, charisma, and fortune, so if you wish to use these qualities in some way, then it would be appropriate to make a planetary talisman for the Sun.

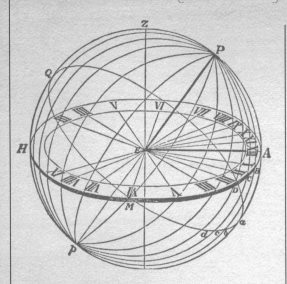

A note about Saturn, Jupiter, and Mars

The following pages give the kameas, planetary seals, and related information for the planets. You will notice that those for Saturn, Jupiter, and Mars are omitted. This is because the spirits associated with those spheres are extremely difficult to connect with for talismanic purposes. Those of Mars are dangerous because they are difficult to control, and those of Jupiter and Saturn are too remote and abstract from a human point of view for any but the most experienced and skillful mages to be able to engage with successfully.

TIMING CALCULATIONS

Planetary days

Sun = Sunday
Moon = Monday
Mercury = Wednesday
Venus = Friday

Sequence of planetary hours

Sun

Venus

Mercury

Moon

Saturn

Jupiter

Mars

TIMING

The talisman should be constructed on the correct day and at the correct time. The sequence of the planetary hours is shown on page 75, but how do you apply this sequence to the hours of the day? There are various systems, but for many the most satisfactory is a flexible system beginning at the moment of sunrise on Sunday.

If the Sun rises at 6:35, the hour of the Sun (the planet that corresponds with Sunday) is from 6:35 to 7:35, followed by the hour of Venus until 8:35, then Mercury, the Moon, Saturn, Jupiter, and Mars. The sequence then repeats until sunrise on Monday morning, which coincides with the hour of the Moon (the planet that corresponds with Monday), and so on. The last hour before sunrise will be a little longer or shorter than 60 minutes to accommodate the lengthening or shortening of the days.

Fashioning a Sun talisman

This example explains how to make a Sun talisman, but the same method can be used to make other planetary talismans. All the necessary information for making Venus, Mercury, and Moon talismans is on pages 126–127.

Sun

Make a Sun talisman for matters relating to health, ego, creativity, superiors, success, advancement, leadership, friendship, growth, and light.

Hebrew name: Shemesh

Day: Sunday

Color: Gold

Complementary color: Purple

Number: 6

Divisions in kamea: 36

Sum of row or column: 111

Sum of diagonal: 111

Spirit of the Sun: Sorath (ThRVS in Hebrew)

Numerical sequence of spirit: 4, 20, 6, 6

Intelligence of the Sun: Nakhiel (LAYKN in Hebrew)

Numerical sequence of intelligence: 30, 1, 10, 20, 5

1. On the appropriate day and time (see page 123), make the basic object. Six is the number of the Sun, so the talisman should have six sides and a diameter of six units—for example, 6 in. (12 cm). The talisman should be the appropriate color, which in this case is gold. As for material, that can be anything corresponding to the Sun, such as gold, amber, or walnut wood. The most important factor is color, however, so a piece of cardboard painted gold would be fine.

2. Carve or paint (in black or the complementary color) the kamea of the planet onto the talisman.

3. Carve or paint the planetary seal. This is a device that touches all of the numbers on the kamea. The traditional seals are provided here, but some have been adapted over time for ease of use and you will find that they do not in reality touch all of the numbers.

4. Carve or paint the sigil of the intelligence or spirit that you wish to call upon (see page 122). For example, to construct the sigil of the angel Nakhiel, the idea is to convert each letter of the name (spelled LAYKN in Hebrew) into a number using the Aiq Bekar (see page 121), then mark this numerical sequence on the Sun's kamea. Construct the sigil by drawing lines between these numbers in the correct order (see opposite).

Planetary seal of the Sun.

6	32	3	34	35	1
7	11	27	28	8	30
19	14	16	15	23	24
18	20	22	21	17	13
25	29	10	9	26	12
36	5	33	4	2	31

Kamea of the Sun with the sigil of Nakhiel.

6	32	3	34	35	1
7	11	27	28	8	30
19	14	16	15	23	24
18	20	22	21	17	13
25	29	10	9	26	12
36	5	33	4	2	31

Kamea of the Sun with the sigil of Sorath.

5. Carve or paint the objective as concisely and specifically as possible in one sentence—for instance:

"Give me more vitality."

6. If you wish, charge the talisman with a fluid condenser made from an appropriate plant, such as St. John's wort for a Sun talisman (see pages 58–61). When completed, wrap the talisman in silk and store it safely before consecrating it. The consecration should also take place on the correct day and at the correct time, perhaps a week later. There is no fixed formula for consecrating talismans; you must construct your own rite once you have become well versed in all aspects of ritual. The most important thing is to focus your intent and channel your will into the talisman. If all goes well, the talisman should prove effective within a week, and like any well-prepared magical implement, it may sustain its influence indefinitely.

DRAWING THE SIGILS

You will sometimes find that a number in the Hebrew name of a spirit or intelligence does not appear on the kamea. For example, the Hebrew name for Nakhiel is LAYKN, which corresponds to the numbers:

30   1   10   20   50

The number 50 does not appear on the Sun's kamea, so use the trick of reducing it (no more than necessary) until it fits. Therefore, 50 becomes 5 + 0 = 5; the number 5 does appear within the magic square.

A note about sigils

The numerical sequences for the Hebrew names of the spirits and intelligences are provided here, but note that different sequences may be used by other mages and in other traditions. As with the planetary seals, many of the sigils that you may come across will also have become stylized over time. Whatever sigil you use, it is the intent with which you draw it on the talisman that matters more than the specific shape.

St. John's wort

Venus

Make a Venus talisman for matters relating to love, pleasure, female sexuality, the arts, luxury, scent, and social affairs.

Hebrew name: Nogah

Day: Friday

Color: Green

Complementary color: Red

Number: 7

Divisions in kamea: 49

Sum of row or column: 175

Sum of diagonal: 175

Spirit of Venus: Kedemel (LAMDK in Hebrew)

Numerical sequence of spirit: 30, 1, 40, 4, 20

Intelligence of Venus: Hagiel (LAYGA in Hebrew)

Numerical sequence of intelligence: 30, 1, 10, 3, 1

Mercury

Make a Mercury talisman for matters relating to intellect, business, writing, buying and selling, information, wisdom, cleverness, science, and memory.

Hebrew name: Kokab

Day: Wednesday

Color: Orange

Complementary color: Blue

Number: 8

Divisions in kamea: 64

Sum of row or column: 260

Sum of diagonal: Upper left to lower right 175; upper right to lower left 257

Spirit of Mercury: Taphthartharath (ThRThRThPT in Hebrew)

Numerical sequence of spirit: 40, 20, 40, 20, 40, 8, 9

Intelligence of Mercury: Tiriel (LAYRYT in Hebrew)

Numerical sequence of intelligence: 30, 1, 10, 20, 10, 9

Moon

Make a Moon talisman for matters relating to clairvoyance, sleep, dreams, emotions, astral travel, imagination, women's mysteries, birth, and reincarnation.

Hebrew name: Levanah

Day: Monday

Color: Purple

Complementary color: Yellow

Number: 9

Divisions in kamea: 81

Sum of row or column: 369

Sum of diagonal: 369

Spirit of the Moon: Chasmodai (YADVMShCh in Hebrew)

Numerical sequence of spirit: 10, 1, 4, 6, 40, 30, 8

Intelligence of the Moon: Malkah be-Tarshisim we-ad be-Ruachoth ha-Schechalim (MYLChSh ThVChVRB DOV MYSYShRTB AKLM in Hebrew)

Numerical sequence of intelligence: 60, 10, 30, 8, 30, 40, 6, 8, 6, 20, 2, 4, 70, 6, 40, 10, 60, 10, 20, 9, 2, 1, 20, 30, 40

Kamea of Venus.

22	47	16	41	10	35	4
5	23	48	17	42	11	29
30	6	24	49	18	36	12
13	31	7	25	43	19	37
38	14	32	1	26	44	20
21	39	8	33	2	27	45
46	15	40	9	34	3	28

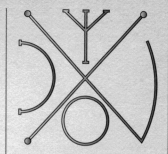

Planetary seal of Venus.

Kamea of Mercury.

8	58	59	5	4	62	63	1
49	15	14	52	53	11	10	56
41	23	22	44	45	19	18	48
32	34	35	29	28	38	39	25
40	26	27	37	36	30	31	33
17	47	46	20	21	43	42	24
9	55	54	12	13	51	50	16
64	2	3	61	60	6	7	57

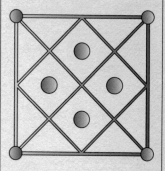

Planetary seal of Mercury.

Kamea of the Moon.

37	78	29	70	21	62	13	54	5
6	38	79	30	71	22	63	14	46
47	7	39	80	31	72	23	55	15
16	48	8	40	81	32	64	24	56
57	17	49	9	41	73	33	65	25
26	58	18	50	1	42	74	34	66
67	27	59	10	51	2	43	75	35
36	68	19	60	11	52	3	44	76
77	28	69	20	61	12	53	4	45

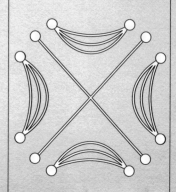

Planetary seal of the Moon.

In classical Indian yoga philosophy, the five elements—earth, water, fire, air, and spirit—are known as tattwas. Colors and symbols have been associated with these fundamental principles for thousands of years and, by contemplating the tattwas, the mage is able to generate shifts in individual consciousness.

Tattwa magic

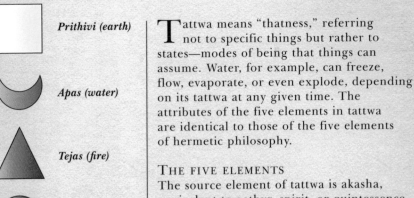

Prithivi (earth)

Apas (water)

Tejas (fire)

Vayu (air)

Akasha (spirit)

Tattwa means "thatness," referring not to specific things but rather to states—modes of being that things can assume. Water, for example, can freeze, flow, evaporate, or even explode, depending on its tattwa at any given time. The attributes of the five elements in tattwa are identical to those of the five elements of hermetic philosophy.

THE FIVE ELEMENTS
The source element of tattwa is akasha, equivalent to aethyr, spirit, or quintessence, from which the four mundane elements emerge. Vayu, the principle of air, mediates between the primary elements of fire and water, the first polarity in the materializing world. From the interaction of these three principles, prithivi, or earth, emerges as the principle that coalesces all the preceding elements, giving them a solid form.

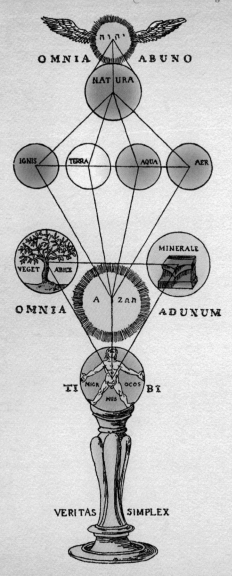

OMNIA ABUNO

NATURA

IGNIS   TERRA   AQUA   AER

MINERALE

VEGET ABILE

OMNIA   A ZΩΛ   ADUNUM

TI   MICR OCOS MUS   BI

VERITAS   SIMPLEX

The relationship of the elements in hermetic philosophy, from *Secret Symbols of the Rosicrucians*, 1785, a compendium of alchemical and mystical wisdom.

CREATIVE AND DESTRUCTIVE POLARITIES

All four lower elements contain a polarity within them, one of which is creative and the other destructive. Fire is electric; it provides light and warmth, but it also burns. Water is magnetic; its active pole is nourishing and protective, but its negative pole dissolves and ferments. Air takes its qualities from both of the primary elements—warmth from fire and humidity from water. It is the midwife that delivers the earth principle that acts as a magnet and contains the preceding elements within itself.

Tools of awareness

Despite the emphasis on the elements in high magic, little useful literature is available to help the aspiring mage understand his or her essential nature on a practical level. The tattwa elements come into their own in this respect, because the colors and symbols associated with them work on a primal level. They can be used as meditational tools that trigger responses within the individual, generating experiences that lead to increasing awareness of how the elements operate in correspondence with all levels of being, right up to transcendence of individual consciousness.

Tattwa cards

The tattwa symbols are easy to use. They can be painted onto plain cards and used in daily exercises and meditation (see pages 132–133).

Making the cards

1. Cut out 25 white cards, 4–6 in. (10–15 cm) square, one for each tattwa element and subelement.

2. Gather ten brand new paintbrushes and a set of ten rich bright paints, such as artist's acrylic paints. You will need the five tattwa colors (yellow, silver, red, blue, and indigo) and five complementary background colors (purple, black, green, orange, and greenish yellow).

3. Using a new brush for each color, paint the cards in the appropriate colors and shapes (see opposite). It is easiest to do the backgrounds first and paint the colored symbols on afterward, making sure that the background is completely dry first.

Prithivi (earth) cards

Apas (water) cards

Tejas (fire) cards

Vayu (air) cards

Akasha (spirit) cards

Prithivi (earth)

Earth, or prithivi, is represented by a yellow square. Although the color differs from the traditional Western correspondence (which is white, black, or brown), you should be familiar with the square, which is analogous to the number four, representing physical manifestation and solidity. For meditational purposes, paint the yellow square on a purple background, purple being the complementary color of yellow.

Apas (water)

The principle of water, or apas, is represented by a silver crescent Moon. This symbol is apt because the Moon controls all liquid activity on the planet. The Moon is also magnetic and containing. Its element, water, is represented by the mage's cup. Half fill a test tube with water, and you will see that the surface is convex, the liquid appearing to be drawn up the sides of the glass like this tattwa symbol. The complementary color of silvery apas is black.

Tejas (fire)

Like the hermetic alchemical symbol for fire, tejas, the principle of fire, is depicted by an upward-pointing equilateral triangle, suggesting its volatile, ascending nature. The color of this triangle, as in Western esotericism, is red. Its complementary color is green.

Vayu (air)

When the great vault of the sky is empty, it appears perfectly blue and arches over the Earth as if it is contained in a great bowl. It consists entirely of air. The tattwa symbol for vayu, the principle of air, is therefore a blue circle. Its complementary color is orange.

Akasha (spirit)

Akasha is sometimes called space; it is the matrix that provides room for the other elements to emerge and establish material life. It is the source, the mysterious origin of all things. In this sense it is like a womb and its symbol suggests as much, being a black or indigo oval like an egg. As a tattwa card, paint the symbol indigo on a greenish-yellow background.

Use tattwa cards as an aid to meditation.

The subelements

In tattwa, the five elements can be subdivided into twenty subelements. For example, earth, or prithivi, has its earthy aspect (hard and heavy like iron), its fiery aspect (volatile like explosives), its watery aspect (fluid like mud), and its airy aspect (light, like styrofoam). The symbols of the subelements are simply the main element symbol with a smaller version— the "seed"—of the aspect element within it. For example, the airy aspect of earth is depicted as the blue circle of air within the yellow square of earth on its purple background.

Card exercises

You can incorporate tattwa card exercises into your daily routine in the morning and evening. Do not do too much too soon—these powerful tools can easily give you headaches and other disturbances if abused.

Palming exercise

Start with the five main elements, beginning with prithivi, then apas, tejas, vayu, and akasha. Just one a day will suffice to start with. Then move on to include the subelements, perhaps working with all five cards of each element on the same day, again starting with prithivi.

When doing any tattwa card exercise, record all the details of the experience in your magical diary, noting your mood before and after.

1. *Perform the lesser banishing ritual of the pentagram to clear the space (see pages 64–65). Sit on the chair in your temple facing the direction corresponding to the card you have chosen. Prop the card on the altar or attach it to the wall at eye level. Stick a piece of white paper next to the card (a white wall is fine).*

2. *Palm your eyes as described on page 21 (step 1).*

3. *Gaze at the tattwa card in a relaxed but alert manner for a couple of minutes or until a pronounced rim aura appears. The image may even start to flash. Shift your gaze to the blank card, paper, or wall. You will see that your mind's eye transfers the shape of the symbol onto the white space, but in the complementary color. The yellow square of prithivi will therefore appear purple. Hold it for as long as you can, then palm your eyes.*

4. *Having worked with all the cards, try to memorize and visualize them in their true colors and complementary colors. This can be done while palming the eyes.*

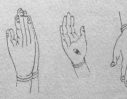

Card meditation

1. *Sit facing the direction of the element in question. Visualize the complementary image of the card and intensify it, then expand it to the size of a door. Imagine your astral body passing through this door, leaving your physical body behind.*

2. *Once through the door, pause to observe the new space you find yourself in. With practice, you may find yourself being able to move into this new vista and interact with the phenomena you find there. Be sure, however, to return through the tattwa door.*

3. *Imagine your astral body reinhabiting your physical body. Then imagine the tattwa door you have returned through reverting to its normal color, symbolizing the closing of the door to the elemental astral realm.*

4. *Perform the lesser banishing ritual of the pentagram (see pages 64–65).*

Once you are able to visualize any card at will after practicing the palming exercise (see opposite), you can then start meditation work. The aim of this practice is to use the complementary images of the tattwa symbols as doorways into the elemental realm. Begin with the prithivi card, then the other elements, followed by the subelements.

Tattwa meditation involves projecting your astral body into the elemental realm.

TATTWA DIRECTIONS

Prithivi (earth) = north
Apas (water) = west
Tejas (fire) = south
Vayu (air) = east
Akasha (spirit) = center of altar

Mahayana Buddhism contains some of the oldest and most highly developed paths of magical attainment known to the world. Its highest masters reincarnate again and again to develop the teachings and help their fellow beings transcend samsara, the wheel of life. The diamond thunderbolt path is one method of transcending the wheel.

The diamond thunderbolt path

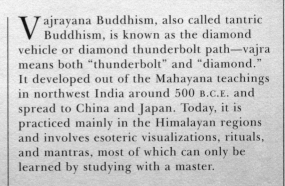

Vajrayana Buddhism, also called tantric Buddhism, is known as the diamond vehicle or diamond thunderbolt path—vajra means both "thunderbolt" and "diamond." It developed out of the Mahayana teachings in northwest India around 500 B.C.E. and spread to China and Japan. Today, it is practiced mainly in the Himalayan regions and involves esoteric visualizations, rituals, and mantras, most of which can only be learned by studying with a master.

UNION WITH THE DIVINE

Emphasis is placed on attaining union with the divine by developing magical powers and abilities. In the Vajrayana path, all situations can and should be used as part of the spiritual journey. The word "tantra" means "continuity," implying that no division exists between sacred action and secular action.

CHANNELING SEXUAL ENERGY

Vajrayana teaches not to suppress energy but rather to transform it. Some aspects of tantra dealing with sexual yoga were assimilated into certain Western magical organizations in the late nineteenth century. These consist of techniques for retaining and channeling sexual energies. To these primarily physical techniques were added various rituals designed to consecrate the sexual act and honor the sexual partner as a god or goddess, thereby reenacting the sacred act of creation.

Tantric Buddhism includes physical techniques such as channeling sexual energy.

Warning

Masters of the diamond thunderbolt path believe that, without a clear motive to help others and a strong grounding in meditation, practicing tantra is dangerous and ultimately self-destructive.

Chanting mantras

All forms of Mahayana Buddhism use mantras as a key part of their daily practice. Mantras are phrases or series of phrases that are chanted repeatedly. These chants are usually monotonous, with perhaps one or two other notes punctuating them. Mantras are essentially magical incantations. The words "chant," "incantation," and "enchantment" all come from the same Latin word meaning "to sing." The aspiring mage soon learns the power of vibrating certain words and phrases.

HOW MANTRAS WORK

Mantras are nothing other than extended invocations. The vibrational qualities of certain sounds, particularly when repeated over and over, alter the electromagnetic frequency of the mage, attracting those forces whose vibrational signature they bear. The essence of a mantra is emptiness. Chanting it flushes all impurities out of the system, which is important in helping you remove obstacles that might otherwise hinder you on the path. Chanting also frees you from any psychic disturbances that may affect you, protecting you from outside interference and inner resistance. Chanting a mantra daily is greatly encouraged.

The hundred-syllable mantra

Mantra

"Om vensa sattva samaya—manupalaya—vensa sattva tenopa—tishta dri dho me bhava—suto khayo me bhava—supo khayo me bhava—anurakto me bhava—sarva siddhi me prayatsha—sarva karma sutsa me—tsittam shriyam kuru hum—ha ha ha ha ho—hagavan—sarva tartagata—vensa mame muntsa—vensa bhava maha—samaya sattva ah"

Translation

"Om Vajrasattva [one of the five Buddhas], please keep your vows. Vajrasattva, empower [reside in] me and make me firm [in my Buddha nature]. Make me satisfied. Be favorable, be nourishing for me. Grant me all the magical attainments. Indicator of all karma, make glorious my mind."

"Hum! Ha! Ha! Ha! Ha! Hoh!"

[Hum is related to om, amen, and omni—everything. Each Ha represents one of the four elements. At the end of the last Ha, take a breath. Hoh is considered the most joyful sound in the universe and is vibrated on a higher note.]

"Blessed one, diamond of all the Tathagatas [Buddhas], do not forsake me; make me as a diamond. Great being of the vow AH!"

[The final Ah should be extended, falling in tone at the end.]

This is one of the key mantras of Vajrayana. Its principal purpose is repentance. The mantra helps to wipe the slate clean of the consequences of previous actions, and to dissolve karma by purifying the individual on every level. The mantra is written here phonetically, with dashes marking the rhythmic phrasing, followed by a rough translation.

HOW TO SAY THE MANTRA

The meaning of the words is of less importance than their vibrational power, but a rough translation is provided. There are also some tips on how to say the mantra. It is worth making every effort to get it right, but keep in mind that it is chanted in various ways in different parts of the Himalayas without apparent variation in effect.

Tibetan initiatic meditation

The following teaching, the white lotus, is taken from the Bde-Mchog Tantra, which was first translated into English in 1919, in part by Kazi Dawa Samdup, who also helped translate the Tibetan Book of the Dead into English. The aim of this meditation is to free the mind of its own imagery on the path toward achieving shunyata, a state that transcends even nirvana. Shunyata means, literally, "emptiness." It is the state of absolute freedom, within which anything is possible. It corresponds to vajra, being the diamond mind of pure activity.

The white lotus

This translation is freely based on the original English translation. As the radiant, incorruptible essence of all things, vajra corresponds to Kether, the crown of the kabbalistic tree of life. The supreme devata (god) can be thought of as Kether; the vajra couple as Chokhmah and Binah; Heruka and his consort as Chesed and Geburah; and the other devatas and beings as the lower sephiroth. Hum can be imagined as the word of God, and the bindi as the sound of the absolute being.

1. *Imagine your navel as an eight-petaled white lotus. In its center is a lunar disk, upon which are Vajrasattva (the personification of the diamond thunderbolt) and his consort in ecstatic union, the mantra "Hum" in their hearts.*

2. *Imagine rays of light pouring forth from the Hum in all directions, creating a space that you define as the supreme devata, a vessel containing the other gods and divine beings. Focus intently on this image. Then imagine that the rays of light issuing from the Hum energize all these beings, activating them, just as a magnet excites iron dust into activity.*

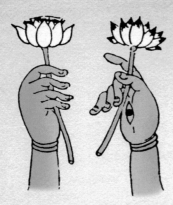

In Buddhism, the lotus is a symbol of purity. Its unfolding petals represent pure beauty and expanding consciousness.

Circular designs, or mandalas, are used as meditational tools. Many feature lotus patterns.

3. Then the rays begin to draw back in, taking with them the vessel of light and all its contents, absorbing them into the form of Heruka (the chief external deity) and his consort, just as mercury absorbs particles of gold.

4. Next, the consort of Heruka is absorbed into the male, the two becoming one face and two hands.

5. Then Heruka is absorbed into the vajra couple on the lunar disk at the heart of the lotus.

6. Next, Vajrasattva's consort sinks into the male, then gradually the male dissolves into the Hum in the heart and the Hum slowly resolves itself into the bindu (point). Finally, the bindu recedes, becoming smaller and fainter until it fades away completely as salt dissolves in water.

Hindu and Buddhist deities are often depicted sitting on a lotus flower. The cross-legged position, with each foot on the opposite thigh, is known as the lotus position and can be adopted to aid meditation.

Index

Bibliography

- *The Alchemist's Handbook*, Frater Albertus
- *The Book of the Sacred Magic of Abra-Melin*, S.L. MacGregor Mathers
- *The Book of Thoth*, Aleister Crowley
- *The Complete Golden Dawn System of Magic*, Israel Regardie
- *A Dictionary of Angels*, Gustav Davidson
- *A Dictionary of Symbols*, J.E. Cirlot
- *A Garden of Pomegranates*, Israel Regardie
- *How to Learn Astrology*, Marc Edmund Jones
- *How to Make and Use Magic Mirrors*, Nigel R. Clough
- *I Ching: The Book of Changes*, James Legge edition
- *An Illustrated Encyclopaedia of Symbols*, J.C. Cooper
- *Initiation into Hermetics*, Franz Bardon
- *The Inner Structure of the I Ching*, Lama Anagarika Govinda
- *Inner Traditions of Magic*, William Gray
- *Kundalini Yoga for the West*, Swami Swivananda Radha
- *The Ladder of Lights*, William Gray
- *Magick*, Aleister Crowley, edited by John Symonds and Kenneth Grant
- *The Mystical Kabbalah*, Dion Fortune
- *Planetary Magick*, Melita Denning and Osborne Phillips
- *The Practical Handbook of Plant Alchemy*, Manfred M. Junius
- *The Practice of Magical Evocation*, Franz Bardon
- *Secret Power of Tantrik Breathing*, Swami Sivapriyananda
- *A Self Made by Magic*, William Gray
- *The Shining Paths*, Dolores Ashcroft-Nowicki
- *The Tarot*, Paul Foster Case
- *The Way of the Sufi*, Idries Shah